Midlife Clarity

Midlife Clarity

Epiphanies from Grown-Up Girls

Edited by
Cynthia Black and Laura Carlsmith

BEYOND
WORDS
Publishing
I N C

Beyond Words Publishing, Inc.
20827 N.W. Cornell Road, Suite 500
Hillsboro, Oregon 97124-9808
503-531-8700
1-800-284-9673

Editor: Laura Carlsmith
Managing editor: Julie Steigerwaldt
Proofreader: Nelda Street
Design: Amy Stirnkorb Design
Composition: William H. Brunson Typography Services

Printed in the United States of America
Distributed to the book trade by Publishers Group West

Library of Congress Cataloging-in-Publication Data
    Midlife clarity : epiphanies from grown-up girls / edited by Cynthia
Black and Laura Carlsmith.
      p.   cm.
    ISBN 1-58270-076-1 (pbk.)
    1. Middle aged women—Biography.   2. Middle aged women—
Psychology.   3. Middle aged women—Conduct of life.   4. Self-
realization.   5. Self-actualization (Psychology).   I. Black, Cynthia,
1952–   II. Carlsmith, Laura.
HQ1059.4 .M53   2002
305.244—dc21

                                                      2001056555

The corporate mission of Beyond Words Publishing, Inc.:
Inspire to Integrity

Contents

At about age thirty-five, something begins to click in a woman's brain. She may notice it on a conscious level or may have only a niggling feeling.... Not everyone lets it in ... You might hear her husband comment, "This is not the woman I married! She would never have said that or done that in the past." That's when I say, "You go, girl!"

In that small, blood-red lump I saw proof of a power in my own body to make and give birth to life. I was a woman. And yet, this was not the mystery of creating I longed for most. I knew then with my whole heart that I would have to choose.

At 4:50 P.M. I turn off the computer and leave the claustrophobic cube of yet another temp job assignment. I am premenopausal, my mood swinging like a metronome. Between the hot flashes, night sweats, and uncontrollable emotional outbursts that have alienated a couple of family members and a coworker, it seems like a good time to quit smoking.

I've always wanted to do this self-exploration thing. I've read all the books and articles and watched Oprah daily to help me get started. . . . all the "helpings" of Chicken Soup for the Soul—all purported to be uplifting, fulfilling spiritual guidance into a world that will make your life complete. "Yeah right," I whisper. "How come I'm not feeling 'spiritual' or 'complete'? I think I'll write a book someday and call it 'Vegetable Soup for the Soul, Made from the Carcass of Life.'"

My new life might have started with a zebra. . . . The white stripes represented the traditionally feminine traits of submission and supportiveness. . . . They were beautiful. But those black stripes, stripes of independence and aggression, in combination with the white, were what gave the animal her unique sense of harmony and balance. . . . I wasn't yet thinking about how one-sided and discordant my own life was. But an unconscious part of me knew, "I want to be white and black too."

I've climbed the highest heights, sailed the bluest oceans, ridden the swiftest horses, kayaked the whitest rivers, marathoned on foot and pedal. And for what? The challenge? The adventure? . . . No! No! No! I did it all for the costumes, the outfits, the "look."

Doing things with awareness, experiencing times of serenity and happiness and harmony—somehow they get inside of you and become part of who you are and what people see in you.

Some delicate fiber ran between my mother and me, connecting us. A fine spider silk that vibrated gently as if touched by a breath or the tip of a finger, sending messages to be transcribed by the receiver. And so I knew, before the signs became evident, before the diagnosis was made, that she was dying—knew by the quivering of the thread.

When it's time to check out, I don't look for the shortest line. Oh no, that's not the way a big-game shopper does it. No, the shortest line is for all those cute little gals with their handbaskets. If you have two baskets, like me, you look for the checker who shows the least fear. You've got to look them in the eye and make sure they see what they're up against. If it looks like they're up to snuff, you take them on.

Sometimes I wish I had a sign with the word "Information" circled in red with a bar going through it that I could hold up whenever I am about to be assaulted by information I'd rather not have.

I realized that my husband had inadvertently revealed himself to me.... *As long as you buy orange juice, Mary, I'm going to drink it.* In one terse statement, he had served notice to me that not only would he not be involved in making a decision but that he had no qualms about sabotaging mine.

The more I watched her watch me, it became clear that this coyote had something I didn't—a perpetual hunger pang and plenty of time on her paws to appease it. She was here to stay. Even worse, I sensed she knew I did not have time on my side today. It was as if the coyote had staked out these acres before. She knew the rhythm of my life.

I talked to my body on Saturday
You know, for a long time we weren't friends
Now that I look back
I'm not sure why

Knowing who we are makes finding the road to travel easier. Direction signs, lane markings, and the yellow dotted lines show up. So do closed tunnels and washed-out bridges, and every now and then, a stop sign appears. Knowing where to park is a good thing.

I have enormous personal power, which brings me to a key point for all of us. What caused women to turn away from our role in the home was not the work. It was power. We needed power. And we came to believe that the way to get power was to do what men do. But that's a lie we've seen exposed by the millions of women passed up for promotion or sexually harassed.

Grief had knocked me down—and kept me down—before it forced me to rebuild. . . . I came to realize that laying this foundation will involve diligence for the rest of my life. But I know now what its cornerstone is for me—acceptance. Given the acceptance by ourselves and others that we, as grieving people, are OK—we are not crazy—our grieving souls can then begin to heal.

My male consciousness didn't rise until . . . my son was born. It was then that I realized no true human equality could be achieved until men challenged the shackles that bound them too, and men and women decided to raise their boy children differently. I . . . had a chance (albeit a very tiny one) to bring humankind closer to real equality. It began with me, a mom raising a son.

"How can you let go of *this*?" some well-meaning friend would wail. "It's just stuff," I said. "I've enjoyed it. Now someone else can." We were moving in order to enjoy the mountains, to hike and ski while we still had health and strength, not to dust our stuff. These things I had been hoarding had no place in that new life.

"Dig, dig, dig!" Betsy hollered when the raft fell into a deep hole. I shouted "Yahoo!" as we rode white water that thrilled me as much as any roller-coaster ride. Suddenly, I was transported into the air as softly and effortlessly as a feather on the wind. I felt as though I were in a dream—I was not where I was supposed to be.

An early empowering moment came when a male seminary professor asked about my theology, responding to my feminist statement with, "Oh, special-interest theology." I somehow took unfamiliar courage and responded, "*All* theology is special interest. You need to acknowledge the presence of *your own* special interest."

Today was the twenty-fifth anniversary of the loss of my virginity. The event itself was not one to be celebrated (or even, if given the choice, recalled) but the milestone is worthy of recognition, I feel.

When I choose to see my life as art and surrender to the process, I find that my work flows; it fills me with energy, rather than draining me. When I first began [quilting] I planned each piece before I began stitching. Then I spent countless hours trying to make the quilt fit the image. Experience has since taught me to work intuitively and to listen. . . . Each piece has a message of its own . . . the final image may be radically different from the spark that created it.

I am willing to bet that if Eve had had a good girlfriend during her reign in the Garden of Eden, undoubtedly the girlfriend would have influenced Eve's decision to partake of the apple, thus altering the history of the world.

Although I hadn't driven stick for years, it was instinct—I was going to *drive*—not chauffeur, not shuttle. My destination was nowhere—not a practice, a lesson, or the store. I was at one with the road.

I did not feel this faith in my thirties and forties. The agendas of life were too immediate, too important. My motivation to reach some unseen goal was too great. I used to believe that without the usual reactive displays of emotion, I would not feel a true connection in my life. Now I try to remember the daily practice of silent reflection and prayer.

I decided long ago that I was going to laugh often, win the respect of intelligent people and the affection of children, appreciate beauty, find the best in others, and leave the world a little better than I found it. To know that even one life has breathed easier because I have lived—this, to me, will be my success.

In this last third of my life, I have found my laugh. Finding it was like finding a complete shell on the beach. It has been part revelation and part discovery but always cathartic and joyous. Somewhere deep inside me now is the "knowing."

Perhaps I and anyone else with a disability—whether physical, emotional, or mental—when faced with a new person or situation in our lives, are in a sense dealing once more with an old question we like to think is long buried, but which in reality we never did resolve: *Will I be accepted and liked as I was before I became disabled?*

Now if he took care of me with all that urgency and attentiveness I would be one satisfied woman. People would stop me on the street and ask what happened. My grin would be so wide, people would swear I was on something. My eyes would be so bright the addicts would be asking for my contact.

What I am relieved about is that I am still alive; in good health; and very much interested in life's challenges, rewards, and surprises. To ask "What am I supposed to learn from this?" instead of "Why me?" is to die less a fool.

How do you know if your dream is worthy of the work it takes to turn it into reality? One sign is that if it's all uphill, if things eventually don't fall into place, take a second look. Maybe you're dreaming someone else's dream. Or, maybe this dream needs to happen at another time in your life.

A fine line to navigate, this life divided between joy and sorrow. The task, I think, is to find ways to discover those however-brief intervals of happiness within the layers of life, to open our eyes and really see that it is the simple things, those moments when some ordinary act reveals to us the essential nature and sweetness of life.

Finding clarity necessitates turning the end of your own kaleidoscope. The pieces are all there. The same pieces that were there the last time you looked in the mirror, or last year or last decade, or when you last felt overwhelmed by life.

Introduction

WHO, EXACTLY, ARE GROWN-UP GIRLS? THEY'RE THE women who've figured life out, more or less. They've figured out what exactly in their life needs to be cherished, what requires their dispassionate attention, and what they can dismiss as pure baloney. They are women who've shredded the script they followed when they were younger. They've found a way to get through each day (or most days) without blame, reproach, or anger. Somehow, they've arrived at a fundamental contentment. These women work without whining, not because they're silent martyrs, but because they *choose* to do the work, to exercise their talents, for themselves and for the people in their lives. Some women have their "midlife" moment of clarity at twenty-four; others are fifty, still in a fog of frustration, looking for and holding on to slights, and presenting a pinched face of tension and stress to the world.

This definition of midlife clarity came to us from Jane Foley, who envisioned a book of stories by women who finally "got it"—and who, at midlife, when they were most surrounded by life, arrived at the clearness of vision that can inspire the rest of us, when our lives seem chaotic, filled with minutiae, obligations, and despair. Her vision happily resulted in this book, for which we asked hundreds of women to send us stories of their moment of insight and clarity. From their responses, we have found these gems—some of which made us cry, some of which made us guffaw, and others that seemed as if they could have been written by Everywoman.

We like how one of our contributors, Saundra Thurman-Custis, describes her epiphany and the lesson she gained from it. It came one afternoon as she perched on a kitchen stool, watching her husband passionately massage the finish on his Volvo, and wishing she were getting some of that same tender, loving attention: "When you find yourself unfulfilled, understand that you're only at a turning point. Nurture and develop your gift, get your life back in balance, and determine to maintain that balance."

She and the other grown-up girls in this book will make you laugh out loud or nod in empathy as they coolly appraise their lives (and the people in them) and make the changes they need to make to emerge from the shroud of others' expectations.

For another contributor, Satori Shakoor, her moment of clarity came after a confrontation with a cell phone junkie who was sitting behind her in a movie theater. After a hellish week, during which she endured the effects of rapidly encroaching menopause and nicotine withdrawal, she was hoping for a respite at the movies. Not a chance. After listening to the woman's ringing phone and play-by-play commentary of the movie, she snapped. After a loud and to-the-point confrontation with the woman, she slumped back into her seat, feeling both angry and embarrassed about her outburst, and looking for support from her man. Instead of a comforting hand, she finds rejection: only a stingy baby finger, extended reluctantly. It was then, in the dark theater, she had her moment of midlife clarity. She writes, "I see in that limp, uncharitable finger the truth of our relationship." From that moment on, her life hasn't been the same. (And neither has his.)

For Barbara Helen Berger, her epiphany came at a young age, when she realized, in a sudden flash of insight, that she had to choose between birthing her art or birthing a child.

Sandy Kay Bryant's clarity is almost palpable, as she writes of baking bread in her wood stove: "It matters what I feel and notice: the silky dough beneath my hands, the grain and color of the wood as I feed it to the fire, the light of morning sun slanting through the window and making latticework shadows on the raisin bread recipe. These are healthy moments in the body of my life."

For others, moments of clarity came in the most mundane of places. In the grocery store checkout line, Jeanne Faulkner was maneuvering her two overflowing carts when she realized: "What I've got here is a two-basket life, full of everything and more of some things than most can handle." Emerging from the details of our everyday lives and rising above them to see them in perspective: that's the clarity we need to appreciate what we've got, change what's not right, and laugh at our quirks.

The women in this book, for the most part, are not iconoclasts breaking down societal barriers. Their stories aren't about fixing lives that were broken. They're about women evolving into their best selves: women pulsing with lives of their own choosing. They've inspired us to laugh, to strive, and to be true to our gifts and our goals. We hope they'll also make you laugh, cry, and appreciate what it is about your own life that is clearly wonderful and unique.

Cynthia Black and Laura Carlsmith

Jane Foley

Midlife Clarity

Jane Foley has worked as a sonographer for over twenty-three years. Such intimate work with people's bodies somehow causes them to spill their hearts and souls as she examines their insides. From years of heartfelt discussions over fearful, hopeful, and joyful times, Jane has learned a lot about the human condition that stretches far beyond the physical body.

Jane grew up in southern California. She took off at the age of twenty-four to work in Saudi Arabia for a few years and then moved to England, where she lived for three years. She now resides on the island of Maui. She is also an accomplished musician and composer.

IT HAPPENED RIGHT BEFORE MY VERY EYES! I HAD unexpectedly popped in to check on a friend who was struggling with many aspects of her life. Just the day before, her teenage son had bent the family car for the third time, Mr. Wrong was caught in his ninth lie, and the child-support check had not come—again.

1

"How are you doing?" I asked, noticing there was something different about her today. She vented about that day's new problem, which I think had something to do with cash flow or, more specifically, the lack of it. I reminded her of a trick my ninety-two-year-old grandmother had taught me. Whenever I complained about an insurmountable problem, she would say, "Put yourself one year forward in time and ask, 'Will this matter next year? Will I even remember it?' Listen to an old lady, and know that nine times out of ten it won't!"

While she digested my grandmother's advice, I paused, and then added, "You know, girl, after forty-eight years, need I remind you of that old adage—God never puts more on your plate than you can handle."

She sat for a long moment, then looked me straight in the eye and said, "Right now I'm very clear about one thing: I need a smaller plate!"

She sat smiling in contemplation for a while before she again spoke. "I think most people would call what I'm going through a midlife crisis, but they're wrong!" She almost shouted as she sat straight up in her chair. "This is not a midlife crisis, this is *midlife clarity*!" The voice that made this announcement was strong, confident, and clear, almost as if a new person had appeared behind my friend's desk. It seemed as if a butterfly had just emerged from the confines of its cocoon and taken flight. She leaned back in her leather chair with a new air of poise and self-reliance, as her eyes wandered upward in thought.

Midlife clarity? She hadn't been clear about anything in her life for a long time, I thought, as I sat observing what was almost a physical change wash over her. In the past year she seemed to have completely lost herself: divorce, single motherhood with two teens, great challenges with her profession, a current dysfunctional relationship, and an ex-husband continually hauling her into court. I guess this was why she wanted a smaller plate, I thought, laughing to myself.

We had been friends for twelve years, casually and professionally, yet for some reason our lives had only recently begun to interconnect on a regular basis. Why now, I had wondered, would our relationship grow close after so many years? I soon found out, as our lives continued to weave together until I found myself hovering on the edge of her midlife whirlpool, strategically poised to throw her a lifeline—the kind of lifeline that can only be thrown from someone in the sisterhood, the lifeline we women earn after weathering many storms.

I returned my attention to her. The moment—yes, at forty-two I remembered my own well. The lifeline I had been attempting to throw her had been earned through years on my own journey of self-discovery, struggle, and, at one point, truly losing myself. Just like my friend in her own whirlpool, I too had navigated through waters I never belonged in to find midlife clarity. Afterwards, I began to see other women move along the same course I had navigated in my thirties, when I found that core essence of "who I am" and began to be comfortable with myself. My "who I am" moment was that same moment my friend was experiencing now: a moment of clarity—midlife clarity!

My thoughts turned to memories of my life before my "moment." I had met a wonderful British man when I was working in the Middle East. We had connected on a level that was that once-in-a-lifetime love. Wow, it was wonderful! I remember thinking, "I now know what it's like to be walking on air." After a few years in the Middle East, we moved to England. As an American, I was enchanted by its tradition, history, and beauty. I made girlfriends and slotted neatly into the English life. What I couldn't see was that, piece by piece, I was slowly losing myself. The more time passed, the more of who I was faded into my fiancé's life. I couldn't work, as a foreigner in another country; I didn't have my American girlfriends; and my fiancé's world began to develop into my own. I didn't know it but I was lost.

It wasn't until I returned to the United States that I realized how lost I really was, not until I began to interact with my girlfriends and feel the early signs of empowerment. The sisterhood to the rescue! It took about three years to regain myself, with the help of my friends. And then the moment came—and it came with a bang! Nothing specific set it off, it just came.

Midlife clarity is a process that usually begins in one's thirties and culminates when you wake up one morning, look in the mirror, and see yourself. Not the self you saw yesterday or the self you saw when you were in another country or the self of the last decade. You see yourself stripped of all the trappings of other's expectations, ambitions, or dreams, liberating your core essence. There is no asking, "Who am I?" You know. You stand tall, you walk proud, you command respect, and you instill confidence in yourself and others. It's clarity, exponentially cubed! You are no longer overwhelmed by life; you are instead wonderfully *surrounded* by it, capable of handling most of what life can deal out.

Surrounded by life! This is what midlife should make you think; yet, all too often, midlife has the stigma of crisis attached to it: "My milestone birthday," "I'm over the hill," "I'm having a midlife crisis," "I'm so old," or "God, I'm depressed; I've really done nothing with my life" are comments commonly heard from women approaching forty.

The word *midlife* can conjure anxious thoughts of that pension plan you're going to start tomorrow, a lost youth, or even of your own mortality. Then the moment comes when you realize, this is the point in life we all long for, not dread: the point where you find yourself braver than you ever believed, stronger than you ever knew, and willing to clarify the rules you now play by to anyone who crosses your path. It's groundbreaking!

You may be driving in your car, sitting quietly at your desk, or drowning in that whirlpool that sucks you down and around so that you feel there is no way out. Oprah spoke about "that moment." She, like so many others, said it's as if a lightbulb just came on. Like clockwork, midlife clarity happens, sometimes on a woman's exact fortieth birthday.

For years I have known this process existed. People watching has always been a favorite pastime, and I've noticed that at about age thirty-five, something begins to click in a woman's brain. She may notice it on a conscious level or may have only a niggling feeling. She may feel as if someone had just introduced her as a new member of the family. Those courteous words we are all taught to say, "Nice to met you," could never have rung so true.

Not everyone lets it in, but not letting it in is akin to knowing you need to shed that extra fifty pounds, and then not even trying to lose them. The fear of looking good may be what is stopping you: you may have to fend off offers for dates or feel you must now perform sexually. But if circumstances allow, and if a woman is not afraid of introducing her new self to her old, the process commences. You might hear her husband comment, "This is not the woman I married! She would never have said that or done that in the past." That's when I say, "You go, girl!"

You may be saying, "Yes! I know exactly what you're talking about!" When you've gone through your moment of clarity, you then have a great perception of the early signs of the process in others. That's when you can place yourself in a position that supports, informs, and throws a lifeline when needed, until your struggling friend comes to the moment of her own midlife clarity.

What a privilege to have been in my friend's office to witness this transformation, the moment her own midlife clarity was born. On that special day, it was obvious to me that another stage in the maturation of the human species had just been labeled, a stage that had either gone unacknowledged or was considered a negative rather than the monu-mental, positive facet of human growth that it is! That moment, midlife clarity, is a right of passage just as real and important as puberty.

Let there be no mistake. The moment of midlife clarity is not where easy street rolls out and the world becomes a kinder, gentler place. This is the kick-off of the second half of the game of life. There will still be penalties, intercepted passes, and yes, the quarterback will sometimes get sacked. But then there will the touchdowns, many field goals, and every now and then even a safety.

Play the game. Play it hard, because this is midlife, and what could be better than being surrounded by life?

Barbara Helen Berger

———— ◊ ————

Dishes

Barbara Helen Berger is an artist who began in fine art, having studied at the University of Washington, Yale, and Tyler School of Art in Rome. During a decade of painting and gallery shows, a feminine and symbolic vision developed in her work, which she then carried into children's books. She has now been writing and illustrating books for twenty years. Her titles include a classic bedtime picture book, Grandfather Twilight *(Philomel Books, 1984), and* Gwinna, *a girls' initiation fairy tale (Philomel Books, 1990). For her, the creative process has always been inseparable from her spiritual life. She has explored both Christianity and Tibetan Buddhism with wonderful teachers, both male and female. In her fifties, she has begun circling back to fine art, and is now writing for adults as well. Her personal essays have been published in* Crone Chronicles, Snowy Egret, *and* Healing: 20 Prominent Authors Write About Inspirational Moments of Achieving Health and Gaining Insight, *edited by Lee Gutkind (Tarcher/Putnam, 2001).*

Barbara lives on Bainbridge Island, near Seattle, with trees all around her studio. Her Web site is *www.bhberger.com.*

I STAND HERE AT THE SINK, HOT WATER RUNNING INTO the dish tub. Steam rises to warm my face. Through the window, with its film of unwashed weather, I see that an earlier mist has dissolved between the trees.

What a fine tradition—a window above a kitchen sink. At home, where I grew up, you could see raindrops on the blossoms of our plum tree. We had no machine to wash the dishes then, and our sink was old-fashioned, low enough for girls like my sister and me. Mom wanted us to help. But the sink was full, more often than not, when she came home from work, late in the day, laden with grocery bags and in time to make supper.

She stared at the heaped-up spoons and bowls crusted with Cheerios, juice glasses, and knives smeared with peanut butter. Even now I can see her face as she fumed in silence, gripping the edge of the sink while she ran the water, eyes shut against the steam. A few words exploded, "How thoughtless you children are! How many times do I have to ask?"

My own face burned. Picking up a dish towel, I knew my hands were too late. I couldn't make up for always forgetting, all those hours after school. But it was hard to grasp how a sink full of dirty dishes could be such a last straw. I had no conception of going out to a job day after day, coming home to cook, iron Dad's shirts, fold the sheets, herd us through our homework, hold us all in the arms of endless love, and collapse into bed with no hope of getting up early to write. When we were small, before her outside job, Mom woke at dawn to sit in the precious solitude at her desk. Now her poems would have to wait, month after month, year after year, in the secrecy of her notebook, in a lost room of her soul. I had no idea what that was like. But I knew Mom gave us all she had.

I look down at my own sink now, to the bath of hot water in my dish tub. Five white china plates are covered with swirls of red the color of pickled beets, purple as plums, red as raspberries and wine. But this is paint, not food. I'm standing at the sink in my studio. Across the room behind me, a large canvas sits on an easel. I've been painting an intricate pattern, dabbing first with a rag, then brushing into the random shapes in shades of red that make me think of the secrets of blood inside the body. For days I've been squeezing crimsons from tubes, mixing them with water and polymer medium on these plates. Now I will let them soak awhile. The dried acrylic colors do not dissolve, the water remains clear. In a few minutes the skins of paint will be soft, easy to scrape away.

In the meantime, I will wash the brushes. Who gave me a first taste for mixing colors? It must have been Dad. I remember sitting at a big table in his studio-office, my little sister beside me. He let us use his own tempera paints. He showed us how to swish the brushes in water to keep the colors from turning to mud. The tempera had a smell that made me happy.

When I was thirteen, he took me to Seattle Art on 8th Avenue downtown. We were there for hours, looking at tubes of oil color, canvas boards, wooden palettes, and brushes standing in rows. One after another, Dad took a brush to dab and stroke in the palm of his hand, as if he were painting. I did too and felt the spring of the bristles. He bought me a selection of sizes, flats and rounds with long green handles. The bristles came from hogs, he said, but they were blond as a palomino's mane. I was planning to paint horses.

The occasion was my first real painting class, on Saturdays at Cornish School. I already knew the way on the #10 Mt. Baker bus. I'd studied ballet at Cornish for years by then. The painting class was up

the same three flights of stairs, just down the hall from that big familiar room with its wall of mirrors and the Chopin, always Chopin,
swelling from the piano. This time, I would walk right by it and enter
another world, filled with a forest of easels.

The teacher, Mr. Frolich, had white hair and an accent. He carried
a long tradition of art upon his shoulders. Chopin études oozed in
under the door as we stood at our easels around a still life—lemons on
a rumpled cloth. The dance of our brushes, halting, searching, dabbing
from palette to canvas board, never quite had the grace of Mr. Frolich's
hand tracing the curve of a lemon in the air.

At the end of class, he sent us to the studio sink. "Now you must
clean your brushes. Always respect the brushes." He showed us how.
Rub the bristles on a block of laundry soap. Work up a lather, rubbing
the brush in the palm of your hand. Rinse, and do it again and again
until the lather is free of color.

All colors mingled in that sink. It was one of those deep laundry
tubs made of gray concrete, with a patina of so many layers of splat-
tered paint, they blended into a single scum, forever smelling of soap
and turpentine. I would bend over many laundry tubs like this later in
other art schools. How did they keep the drains clear?

Nowadays, I rub my brushes in a cake of soap that comes in a
round container, like shoe polish. In Western-style lettering on the lid
it says "The Masters Brush Cleaner and Preserver" and shows a man at
his easel outdoors, wearing a hat like a cowboy Monet. "Keeps Brushes
Like New," it says.

Today my lather is magenta. I rub the brush in the palm of my
hand. Magenta fills my life line, my heart line. I rinse again, again, until
the water runs clear, down the drain. Then I rinse out the water jars,
stand the clean brushes on end, and stop to gaze out the window.
I really should wash it this year.

Once, I had a palette made of glass, a square of heavy plate glass from the hardware store. The edges were taped with black electrical tape, and the back coated white with gesso. That was at the university, where I spent most of my time in the School of Art. The whole second floor smelled of linseed oil and turpentine. Many of us who were majors in painting had made ourselves these palettes of glass. They were easy to clean. You scraped the paint away with a razor blade, leaving the mounds of unused color for tomorrow, or later that night. After class hours, a few of us would be there working late, swathed in smoke from our cigarettes, driven to struggle with colors and shapes, learning what it is to be a serious artist, alone with a canvas and questions that seem to have no answer.

One day during class, the words finally formed in my mind around one of these questions. So I went to the painting professor and asked. I don't remember my question, but I do remember his reply.

"What does it matter?" he said. "You will get married, have a bunch of kids, and you'll never pick up a brush again."

He spoke with such finality, my mouth hung open. Then he left the room. A silent explosion swelled inside my chest. My heart began to pound, *No, No.*

If only I could have asked a woman. We heard of a rare few in painting, in those days—Helen Frankenthaler, Georgia O'Keeffe, and sometimes Mary Cassatt, whose fine drawing was given a nod but whose work as a whole was dismissed. She painted mothers and babies. I didn't see one woman professor of painting in that school then, nor anywhere else I studied. There were plenty of gifted young women students, however. Many were art education majors, destined to teach. The professors never took them seriously. Why lavish their wisdom on girls who would only drown themselves in a sea of children?

Should that make a difference? Why should it matter? My professor's words were far from personal; I was almost able to see that. But my face stung as if he had slapped me. Still shaking, I nearly dropped my glass palette as I put it away and gathered my things. I went home to the dorm, ate a few bites of dinner, and went to my job in the cafeteria kitchen.

Wearing oversized rubber gloves, I scraped leftover food off plates that came on a black conveyor belt in endless procession. Apple sauce, mashed potatoes, butter, and peas slid into the garbage. I felt sick.

It wasn't the food that sickened me, but fear. My period was weeks overdue. Every day I had gone to classes with only a vague sense of the unknown in my belly. Now I had to think. Maybe that professor was right. Soon I would have to go to a doctor. And tell my boyfriend, who might or might not want to get married. All at once I saw how wrong he was for me. And a *baby*. Could it be? Could a new life be taking shape inside me, now, this minute?

An image arose in my mind, faded at the edges like a dream. I must have been about four years old, in a nursery school where there was a baby not much bigger than my doll. That baby cried all day and never stopped. I stared at the tiny chest that kept on heaving. The cries cut right through me. There was nowhere to go.

Later on, baby-sitting around the neighborhood, I never had to take care of an infant so small, only little kids who wrestled me to the floor. But even after they'd gone to bed, I felt trapped in the hours that dragged on and on, waiting on strange sofas for parents to come home so I could leave.

Then, after high school, I took a job as a counselor at Hidden Valley Camp. It sounded like fun. They put me in charge of the older girls, nice, lively girls. But I hated it—trapped again, not only in the tent with its bunks, but even out on the grassy field where we played elaborate all-camp games. There was no place to be alone, no time to think or to draw.

Whenever I could, even when I shouldn't have, I ran into the woods with my sketchbook and a longing so fierce, I was sure my whole body must be on fire. I hid in the cool quiet between the trees, in the blank world of a page, questing for vision with my pencil.

People had to look for me too many times. One day, Harry, the head of the camp, called me into his office. Even sitting down he was tall as Abe Lincoln and Paul Bunyan in one. He looked me straight in the eye.

"I'm concerned," he said. "You have an attitude problem. What's wrong?"

I looked down at my hands. How could I tell him? Nothing was wrong with the girls in my tent, or the horses, or Purdy Creek, or even the endless Jell-O and macaroni. I had been so happy there myself, as a child. Now I felt like a caged animal. What was wrong with me?

Something else is burning in my blood.

"I'm sorry, Harry. I guess I'm just not cut out for this."

All I could do was promise to try harder. At night, I drank beer and sang Bob Dylan songs with the other counselors. During the days, lost in the happy, noisy sea of children, I hoped no one could see in my eyes the animal pacing, pacing inside, waiting to be free.

That was when I first began to know that art is more than talent, more than longing, more than hard work. For some, it is an imperative. Where does that passion come from? The power to create is equal in its power for misery. I began to understand my father's rages, his black clouds that often filled our house, for I had now met in myself the strange hellishness of artistic frustration. I could understand my mother's face, too, when she shut her eyes and gripped the edge of the sink a moment, before she hunched into the steam to fight her way through the dirty dishes.

Now, here I was in the dormitory kitchen. Pregnant. How stupid, how careless I had been. Just when I'd come to know the truth of my own life, I would have to give it up.

Leftover carrots and mashed potatoes kept on coming, plate after plate, tray after tray. Then all at once, the ache in my belly grew sharp—something searing and female. I held my breath. A warm ooze began between my legs. I ripped off the rubber gloves, ran to the restroom, and locked myself in a stall.

Red tinted the water in the toilet bowl. A clot floated down, large enough that I knew what it must be, yet small enough, I couldn't be sure. One way or the other, this was the shape of a life beginning to form. I carry the ambiguity with me still.

I never told my mother, but she would have fathomed the flood of relief I felt. She would have wept in gratitude with me. Nature had changed its mind for her daughter who was so young, with so much art before her. In that small, blood-red lump I saw proof of a power in my own body to make and give birth to life. I was a woman. And yet, this was not the mystery of creating I longed for most. I knew then with my whole heart that I would have to choose.

I have not thought of the miscarriage in—how long? It happened more than thirty years ago. It must be the colors today, the shades of red on my painting dishes here in the sink. Inorganic polymers and pigments with names like "naphthol" and "quinacridone" crimson. Nevertheless the warm water has so softened the dried tissues of paint, they lift away with a touch and drift like tender remnants of exotic seaweed. Deep red flotsam of creation.

One by one, I scrub each plate, rinse, and set it to dry in the drainer beside the sink. The china surfaces are blank again, chipped here and there but white as moons. I love these old dishes. They came from our summer cabin long ago.

Ringed with the cry of gulls, we all felt free and spacious there. Dad forgot his deadlines. He settled into the work shed in back with bits of metal and wood from the beach, making sculpture. My sister and brother ran off to build a raft. Mom sat at the walnut table, gazing out the tall front window over moss and rocks to the sheen of water. Silver light washed over her face, over the pages of her notebook— open at last—and lit the yellow pencil poised in her hand. I went out to draw, and closed the door behind me softly.

Later, one day when she and I were talking about the future, my future, I said, "Well, I'm going to be an artist."

She nodded, of course she knew that.

"But I can't be a mother too. I'm not going to have any children."

She smiled at this. "Oh honey, of course you will."

My heart began to pound again, as if under siege. *No.* I wanted to slam the door against my mother's words, against the assumption that clung to the air as it had for generations. For millennia. But I know now it was not a maternal command in my mother's voice. She spoke from joy. An inconceivable joy she did not want her own daughter to be without. All my life I have seen that joy bloom in her face when she looks at any one of her own children, my brother, my sister, me. We are long since grown and that light never wanes. "Of course you will," she said.

But I never did.

I chose the other light. The one I saw when her face was turned to the window. I think some invisible bird was coming to cover her with its wings, a bird of annunciation. In that moment, the breath of poetry poured into her mind. She looked out the window and deeply within at the same time. There was no boundary between her side of the glass and the vastness beyond. I had tasted the same bliss, when the invisible thing came to me with the call of its imperative. I wanted nothing more than to give my own whole and fervent, *Yes.*

I lift my heavy dish tub now. The water sloshes with fragments of paint. I pour it all out through a sieve I keep by the sink for this, to catch the acrylic remnants before they clog the drain. Soon the mesh will be solid, filled with a confetti of paint poured through the years. Then I will buy another one. And anything else my work may need. Who knows how many brushes I've bought and used and worn out? How many tubes and jars of paint? Hundreds. And the paintings conceived and born—on canvas, on paper, for walls, and for books—they too must number in the hundreds.

I marvel at other women, whose art I admire, whose finely crafted words I read, women who live as artist and mother, both. How they do it I can't imagine. But they do. Then, I also think of that young woman who was myself, not much more than a girl and so unsure in everything but this. Where did the certainty come from—to know she had only one strength, not enough for both? She chose. Or rather, something chose in her. She felt it like a force of nature, intense and clear as instinct. Her own nature rose up to seize the rare chance, a moment in culture and history when it was possible at last to make this choice. She wasn't a brave girl. Yet somehow, she rooted her life in the depth from which that knowing sprang. She felt it must be the ground of her being, as true for her as the ground of motherhood in other women.

I lean on the edge of my studio sink to look again out the window. It is late. I will never see a child of mine running in and out between those trees, where sunlight is slanting now into the clearing. But I do hear voices, shrill happy sounds that make my heart leap. It's the neighbor children spilling out of the yellow house down the hill.

Their voices fly up through the trees like birds. My own joy rises to meet them. It rises even in the quiet reflection here—a woman in the dailiness of her work, musing at the window awhile before she gathers her brushes and plates, and turns again to the mystery she carries, and to the labors of birth.

Satori Shakoor

Confessions of a Mad Black Girl, or How I Took a Men-O-Pause

Satori Shakoor is an actor, singer, comedian, and writer. A twenty-year veteran of live performance, she has recorded and toured with George Clinton's Parliament/Funkadelic *as one of the "Brides of Funkenstein." She has worked with David Foster, Sly Stone, and Luther Vandross. As a comedian, she has opened for Joan Rivers, worked at the Improv and the Comedy Store in Los Angeles, and has headlined at Yuk Yuk's in Toronto.*

In 1997, she received a Dora Mavor Moore nomination for Outstanding Performance by a Female for her self-written, one-woman play, Who She Wasn't. *In 1998, she received two Gemini nominations, Best Writing in a Television Comedy, and Best Performance in a Television Comedy for* Thick and Thin.

Her numerous credits in theater, film, and television include Harlem Duet *(Neptune Theatre, Halifax, 2000),* Ain't Misbehavin' *(The*

17

Grand Theatre, London, Ontario, 2001), The Hurricane *(a film by Norman Jewison),* The Famous Jett Jackson, *and* Mom's the Word *(Centaur Theatre, Montreal, 2001).*

AT 4:50 P.M. I TURN OFF THE COMPUTER AND LEAVE THE claustrophobic cube of yet another temp job assignment. I am pre-menopausal, my mood swinging like a metronome. Between the hot flashes, night sweats, and uncontrollable emotional outbursts that have alienated a couple of family members and a coworker, it seems like a good time to quit smoking. This is the beginning of the change of life. My time to venture out into parts unknown, become an adventurous traveler, climb mountains I never dreamed I would climb, be a full-time moneymaking artist. My time to be free. Giving up cigarettes seems a small price to pay for being whole and free, and besides, how bad can a little nicotine withdrawal be?

Four days after I quit smoking, I go with my boyfriend to see *Traffic,* a film about the drug war. I have been asking Winston, a college professor who professes to be spontaneous, to see a movie with me for weeks. When he finally begrudgingly agrees, he sits brooding. A fifty-six-year-old spoiled brat, he sits slumped in the faux velvet seat, his beer gut a corduroy half-moon, rising and falling above the arm rest, with a scowl on his face, as the theater fills before the feature starts. Tonight everything about him bugs me: the way he checks his watch every two seconds, the beer breath Dentyne can't hide, his knee tap-tapping against mine, forcing itself over into my leg space—a Morse code telegraphing that he would rather sit on my couch, clutch my remote, and flick away my shows in search of *America's Most Wanted.*

Without the numbing effects of nicotine, my nerves are exfoliating, wearing me like a loofah body suit. The special effects are so loud I feel like I'm sitting on an airport runway. Everybody sounds like God when they speak. Five minutes into the movie, the addict in me has counted eleven smoking characters, including background extras. Their cigarettes look like big, lit sticks of dynamite. I want to bum one bad.

I'm in hell, trying to match the English subtitles to moving mouths of Mexicans, when a woman and her date distract me. They hustle up to the second-tier balcony and stop at the row behind us. Entering, they climb over ankles, knees, and legs while mumbling a series of "excuse me's" and "I'm sorry's."

In the process of sitting down, they bump my shoulder, Winston's seat, and the back of both our heads. Once seated, they punch off overcoats, rip wrappers off smuggled-in snacks; they bounce, mutter, and instruct—a ransacking soundtrack that clashes with the subtitles and muted colors onscreen.

Then this woman launches a full-out whispering attack on my eardrums. Her whispers are nails on chalkboard in surround sound, drowning out the special effects. "Whiss whiss Michael Douglas, whiss whiss Zeta Jones, whiss married, whiss pregnant, whiss whiss whiss." She just goes on and on, working the only nerve I have left.

I clench my teeth, whip my neck around, and hiss, "Shhhhh!" Drawing back, she's quieted. "Good," I think as I turn back to the screen, "the beast is silent." Seconds later, she's muttering another inane monologue to her mute date. A cigarette could really help me at this point. Instead I ask Winston for his hand to ground me. Holding on, I will myself to transform her whispers into white noise.

The movie finally lulls me in, when I'm startled by a ringing cell phone. *Her* cell phone. "Hello...? Oh, hi." She answers as if we're all in her living room.

I close my eyes and do a sing-song self-talk. "Stay calm, hold on, anyone can forget to turn off their cell phone, Winston has a cell phone, he could have forgotten to turn his off too, she just forgot, that's all."

"I'm at the movies. Yes. *Traffic* . . . TRAF-FICK!" Her voice cuts through my mantra.

That's it. I snap. "I know you ain't gonna talk on your cell phone up in this movie!"

I feel her hand on my shoulder; I see her mouth, "I'm sorry."

"Get your hand off me!" I scream.

She's crawling over knees and legs to reach the aisle where, giving me attitude, she snips, "Who are you?"

Ten rows of people turn to look at me as if I'm the bad guy, including Winston, who's slumped even further down in his seat from embarrassment. I know he thinks I haven't represented my race well, but I could care less that we're the only people of color in the theater. The woman behind me is rude and wrong and I'm representing myself: a premenopausal woman attempting to liberate herself by going through the agony of nicotine withdrawal. Which reminds me that I need a cigarette, which reminds me that I can't have a cigarette; I can never, ever have a cigarette again.

That's it. I explode. "You ain't got no movie etiquette, you selfish bitch! Are you our movie tour guide? I don't need a blow-by-blow anchorwoman description of every damn thing happening on the screen! You should've waited for the movie to come out on DVD, with your cell phone and big bag of illegal potato chips. Skank!"

My rant is a weird hip-hop rap to her lopsided jog down the steps. I yell, "Cell phone junkie!" as she escapes with her wireless to the lobby.

I'm shaking when I reach for Winston's hand again. Where is it? I feel around and find a stingy baby finger crooked for me to take. Rejected, I think, "He knows what I'm going through and he can't support me?" Then in a burst of insight, in my unmedicated state, I see in that limp, uncharitable finger the truth of our relationship.

His days are numbered.

Seven days later and nicotine free, it's five o'clock, after work, and I'm on my way home. I squeeze into a crowded subway car, sucked in and suffocated by a mixture of odoriferous fumes filling the air around me: curry pores, garlic sweat, mustard fingers, coffee breath, somebody's sushi, and cigarettes. My returning sense of smell has been upgraded to first class.

The train snatches us to the next stop and when the doors open a thick, sharp, intense, stench assaults my nose, overwhelming me. It's homeless-person smell, that trademark scent that instinctively causes my upper lip to reach up in an attempt to shield my nostrils. I sniff the source of the smell to a homeless blind man with a ruddy pallor, tapping a cane that looks like a giant cigarette, lit at the tip, and coming straight at me.

It registers vaguely: he's not blind. He tap-shuffles his stench over to me, stops, and waves his uncaned hand in search of something to hold onto, stirring fumes as the train snatches away. Bouncing forward with the motion of the subway car, he brushes against me, branding his odor on my coat collar.

The doors open. I exit, exhale, and breathe, then move as quickly as I can to the broken escalator leading to the northbound trains upstairs. Smelly blind man is in front of me but I can't get around him, way too many people. He asks, "Will you help me upstairs?" Again the niggling sense he's not blind.

I'm stuck between dumping his stinky ass and faking nice for people I don't know. I frown when he puts his dirty hand on my arm, cringing from the grime I see on his swollen fingers.

I want to get this Mother Teresa act over with, so I run up the dead escalator with his hand on my arm like Donovan Bailey in the '96 Olympics. Hanging on, he hula hoops fumes, spray-gunning me and everything around us, while amazingly, he matches my pace in a race to determine which of us is the bigger phony. He can't be blind.

At the top I look for escape; can't, too many people barreling forward, no one moves for us. They probably know his cane is a crutch, something added for pity points. I snatch my arm away.

Then all of a sudden I get a cigarette craving. It's bad, it's real bad, it's bad. The only thing that stops me from buying a pack is the hot flash that hits me. I hear Smelly fake blind man ask me something about taking him somewhere. I scream, "Fuck off!" as I unbutton my coat, and people fade from the subway platform.

The heat licks its way up inside, a fire-breathing dragon, leaving beads of sweat in its path. I'm faint; my emotions are raging, throwing fists at my chest, banging rhythms in my belly—percussionists gone mad in a pit of drums. I tear my coat off, look for air, close my eyes, and wait until it subsides.

I recover and look across the tracks to the southbound platform wall and see a leftover Dennis Rodman "Got Milk" poster. He's sitting there buck naked, lusting at me with a let's-do-the-nasty smile and that milk mustache on his face. Those tattooed, muscled arms, that chiseled chest, those abs, his hand holding the basketball between his legs. Damn! I want Dennis to rebound out of that poster and take me on the tracks. I want him to dribble that basketball so hard down court that we bounce over to smelly fake blind man, and slam-dunk his ass and everything I'm feeling and everything I'm afraid of into oblivion.

The train screeches in, obstructing my view of Dennis–coitus interruptus. As the subway car pulls away, I sit and take one last peek at the "Got Milk" poster, and thank Dennis for taking the edge off that my boyfriend can't. Winston has had a grand total of two erections in the five and a half months we've been together. A virtual Mr. Softee, who climbs on top of me and when he predictably doesn't get hard, rolls off, faces the wall, and dismisses me as if he's the only one with needs.

I would smoke a cigarette and tell myself, I don't measure a man by the quality of his erection, I measure a man by the promises he makes and keeps. Then I'd smoke another one and tell myself that it might be exciting inventing a whole new sexuality.

After four weeks and nineteen packs of cigarettes, I was fed up with this routine. I needed more sensual, more erotic experiences in our lovemaking and less of his phallocentric obsession.

I whisper in his ear, "It's OK, Baby. There are other things that please me. I love massage."

He turns from the wall and says, "There are other things that please me too."

The only predictable thing about the potency pill he's been taking for the last six years is that it's unpredictable. On the one, rare, occasion when the pill worked too well, he lay erect for hours, a fertility symbol making a tent out of my bedsheets, disgruntled, and begrudging me one more ride.

I would smoke a cigarette and numb myself to the buildup of all the little letdowns, inside and outside the bedroom.

We've been arguing a lot lately, over little things that bother us about each other, and ignoring the bigger thing, which is that we really don't like ourselves. A cigarette can't fix that anymore.

I'm jerked back to the present as the train doors bang open at my stop. That's when it hits me that I'm no different than smelly fake blind man back there. I've been faking too, fumbling around in the dark with a cane stuck in my mouth, a dimmer switch on my feelings, looking for a light.

I don't hide the tears that come quick and hard as I hurry home out of the subway station.

Fifteen days after I have quit smoking, Winston is on his way over, but when he gets here we won't be watching *America's Most Wanted*. The thing about not being numb anymore is that I'm very clear. I can see from see to shining see. I can't count on Winston when it comes to no matter what.

When my buzzer rings, I let him in and get straight to the point, "It's over, Winston."

Unbelieving, he says, "Look, I know it was important to you. But come on. You know how expensive it is to take a taxi all the way downtown at six."

"Yes, I know. "Bye, Winston," I tell him and close the door.

For weeks a pillow muffles my cries; it soaks up rivers of tears, becomes a soft shoulder for the buckets of ache and pain I pour, as I let go till the wee hours of morning the too many long years I've lived without loving myself.

◊ ◊ ◊

It's been six months and I've come a long way, baby, one day at a time. The gym is where I go five days a week to deepen my relationship with oxygen. Out of my breath walks a strong, beautiful, healthier body with a joyful spirit that lies about my age.

I change my diet and I'm blessed with energy that I focus and channel into nurturing and life-affirming pursuits. I give up my addiction to temp jobs, which have been a financial crutch and a creative impediment, jobs I have let use me for years in the enhancement of profit for others. When my time is restored, I realize what a slave I've been to it. Always too busy—rarely relaxing—rushing, hustling to get to those few hours of the day that are mine, but that I have been too tired to enjoy. As I teach myself to use and enjoy time, time teaches me to be a better artist and human just being.

I love this Men-O-Pause, where friendships are what I pursue first and foremost with men. I am grateful for the warm and loving friendships I share with powerful women. I feel a peace, as loving myself becomes a journey of courage for the adventurous traveler who ventures into parts unknown, letting go of everything that isn't true.

When I go to Kenya in December I'm going to climb Mount Kilamanjaro, and when I stand at the top of the highest mountain in Africa, I'm going to take a big, deep breath of the air up there and shout, "I AM FREE!"

Barbara Samuels

The Journey

Barbara was born in Dallas, Texas, and currently lives in Kansas City, Missouri, with her fiancé. She is forty-eight years old, and the single mother of two and grandmother of three. Currently employed as the operations manager for the Negro Leagues Baseball Museum, in her spare time Barbara likes to write, cook, read, and fish. Future plans are to excel in her new career, continue her education, and plan for her wedding.

12:01 A.M., JANUARY 18. THE BEWITCHING HOUR. IT IS THE first minute into my birthday and I stand before the bathroom mirror viewing the image of a now forty-eight-year-old woman. This is how I came into the world—naked. My head cocks from one side to the other as if I'm looking for something I know isn't there. Moving closer, I peer into the glass and stare intently. The reflection back is real. It is me. It scares me for a moment what I see.

"Lord, I hope no one comes in here. They'll think I'm sick or crazy or maybe both." I laugh out loud at the prospect of explaining my nakedness at this hour to the man I love, the man who has seen me in my full glory. Would he understand? I doubt it; he's a man after all. They're sometimes out of touch with what *we* do.

I've always wanted to do this self-exploration thing. I've read all the books and articles and watched Oprah daily to help me get started. Iyanla Vanzant's *Acts of Faith*, Robin Norwood's *Daily Meditations for Women Who Love Too Much*, and of course, all the "helpings" of *Chicken Soup for the Soul*—all purported to be uplifting, fulfilling spiritual guidance into a world that will make your life complete. "Yeah right," I whisper. "How come I'm not feeling 'spiritual' or 'complete'? I think I'll write a book someday and call it 'Vegetable Soup for the Soul, Made from the Carcass of Life.'"

Twenty-nine minutes after I began to look at myself—inwardly and externally—and I have yet to begin this spiritual journey. I've planned this trip for months. I packed the bare necessities—books, tissues, and candles. Hesitantly, I unpack. Why am I stalling? Where am I going? What will I find? Unanswered questions at this point. Don't I have it all—beautiful children and grandchildren, loving man, home, good job? I catch my face in the mirror. And, you're not too bad to look at either! So, why am I doing this? I should be doing it for the family that thinks I've lost my mind lately. I wonder where Oprah would go on her spiritual journey? Would she go to the Fiji Islands in her mind, where there are warm sand, blue skies, and gorgeous men feeding her grapes? She could certainly afford that trip, real or imaginary! Those dreams of serenity would suffice for awhile, but my journey must begin here—at home, in the privacy of my bathroom.

Suddenly, I feel like Dorothy in *The Wizard of Oz*, whose topsy-turvy ride over the rainbow taught her the value of holding on to what was near and dear to her right at home. The answer was simple: she clicked her heels three times and she was free. Is that what I want, to be free of life's complications, free of ties that bind me to my physical surroundings?

Here goes nothing. Lighting the scented candles, I begin my version of the rhythmic chant that freed Tina Turner's soul, "Ohmm, nrangay . . . Ohmm, nrangay . . ." I touch fingertips to fingertips and close my eyes. I see nothing and feel nothing. Must not be doing it right. Again, I chant faster with more emotion and, for good measure, click my heels together three times, "Ohmm, nrangay . . . Ohmmm, nrangay . . ." Still nothing.

Slowly, I open my eyes and stare into the mirror. In those deep brown pools I begin to see what I felt—fear. Fear of the unknown, fear of getting old, fear of dying, fear of not accomplishing what I set out to do with my life. Which is what? I don't know. That's the other fear. Tears slowly well in my eyes and my stomach begins to cramp, gripping me like a vice, in order to stop a full-fledged scream. I quickly slap a hand over my mouth to stifle the noise, and I sit on the toilet. With my arms wrapped around me, I rock back and forth, praying for direction and for a peace that couldn't come with words from a book written by someone who doesn't know squat about me or my life.

1:00 A.M. I rely on one particular book of daily meditations, *Acts of Faith*, to guide me as I turn to the passage for January 18. It reads, "*When you concern yourself with doing only what others 'think' you can do, you lay the floor of your prison.*" True, that.

"*When you allow fear* (there's that word again), *competition, or greed to guide your actions, you lock yourself up and throw away the key.*" Well, I am locked in the bathroom. I wonder if that counts.

"*It is our concern over what others say, do, and think about us that imprisons our mind, body, and spirit.*" Maybe there is something to this stuff. I'm always worried about what others think of me and if I'm doing the "right thing." I dare to venture a look into the mirror again to see my image. I smile and the image smiles back broadly. "Do I defy the laws of spiritual nature that say answers to our worries can be found if only we take the time to pray and trust in God?" Yes, I do. Now, God, please don't throw any lightning bolts my way for that statement. I do believe in You and I do trust You, but, I'm only human and I want to discover a new me today on my terms." Is that OK for this one time, God? I hope He heard that earnest plea.

My hands trace the fine lines on my face that spoke of years of worrying about the fate of my children. I am blessed, Lord. They have given me three beautiful grandchildren. Well, one has given me all of them. Humph!! Wish he'd quit doing that.

I vividly remember the first time I held my grandbaby in my arms, when those tiny hands found my face. So soft, so sweet smelling, so real, so me! Heaven had sent me an angel. It was New Year's Day and cold on the outside but warm inside. I was to turn forty a few days later.

I wonder what he'll think of Grandma's tattoo when he's older? I rub the symbolic tattoo that lay on my right breast. The color was still high, a teddy bear reaching for a butterfly. It was a simple and pleasurable act. I turn around to trace the tattoo on my shoulder, a small broken heart with a lightning bolt through it. Each one exposed the rebel in me and told small parts of my life. I smile, remembering my grandmother's look of shock when the "dirt" on my breast was really a tattoo. She began to see me in a whole new light. I know she was thinking, "Did I raise this child, Lord?" Yeah, Grandma, you did. From you I inherited a youthful appearance, a taste for fine clothes, class, and kindness to others.

2:00 A.M. Funny, I'm not tired yet. No one has knocked to enter my sanctuary. I am safe here. I outline my lips with my fingertips and stick out my tongue, recalling the words I've spoken over time. I regret those that have been hurtful and cherish the words that gave hope to someone in need.

Yes, I have a gift of gab. My boys didn't always see it as a gift when I gave the lecture on keeping their rooms clean or taking out the trash or the facts of life. But, it was always a gift to say I love you. Raising my arms above my head, I reflect on the many times those arms held my children when they cried from falling off their bikes or being the victim of unrequited love, of wrapping my man's arms around me simply to feel his skin next to mine, of remembering holding my mother's hand as she lay dying.

3:00 A.M. I begin to cry at remembering one of my fears—dying. What is dying exactly? A trip into another realm called Heaven? I hope so. Lord, I hope so. Please tell me I'll find my grandmother and mother there waiting for me. How sad to come of age and know that life isn't forever. I just knew they would be around to comfort me, and I to comfort them. They were the Rocks of Gibraltar. I am guilt ridden at times, thinking I could have prevented the inevitable. How pompous of me, I know, but when you love someone as much as I loved them, you think you're invincible. Now the invincible one stands butt-naked before a mirror, in search of herself. Perhaps this moment is a testament to them that I must love me first before I can love anyone else. I open *Women Who Love Too Much*. *"Sometimes we grieve when people leave or conditions change or things are removed that we would never willingly surrender, because we cannot yet see the greater good that is coming to us."*

4:00 A.M. The body begins to wane under the pressure of sleep deprivation, but I trek on fearlessly. "There, I said it: fear, the 'F' word!" Wheeew, a new revelation. I've been so afraid to acknowledge that fear does exist in my life. Am I being healed right here under the subdued lighting?

I stretch my legs and bend over to examine the scars achieved as a child. There's the one from the tomcat I was ordered to leave alone. Here's one from the bike I wasn't supposed to be riding in the first place, for fear of getting hit by a car. They are my proud war wounds. I fought to maintain my tomboyishness in spite of my grandmother's penchant for frills and lace. I lost that good fight. Actually gave it up willingly for my first pair of stockings. These legs have carried me up and down many stairs, back and forth through school hallways and hospital waiting rooms.

I swear I've been in this bathroom too long. I'm hearing strains of Barbara Streisand's "The Way We Were" in my head: "*Memories light the corners of my mind. Misty, watercolor memories . . .*" I guess I am stirring up some memories as I contemplate my life.

5:00 A.M. I search for the two strands of gray hairs. Rather than pluck them, I embrace them between my fingers. You know, I earned these two hairs. They are mine, a testament to my fortitude. But if two, three, or four more gray hairs appear, I will welcome each one like a long-lost friend. I think of Martin Luther King and his speech at Clayborn Temple the evening before his assassination. He spoke, "Well, I don't know what will happen now. We've got some difficult days ahead. But it doesn't matter with me now because I've been to the mountaintop."

Thank you, Dr. King, for voicing what I feel. I'm not at the mountaintop yet, but believe I have reached a juncture in my introspective journey in which I must now stop and look at the whole me before I can move on. "Mirror, mirror on the wall. Who's the fairest of them all?" The mirror doesn't answer back, but it need not. For I think I've found the beginning of answers to my fears, to my dreams, to my lot in life.

6:00 A.M. My journey is complete. I cannot see the sun from where I am, but I know that it is beginning to break. It is rising for me, symbolizing my new beginning. My eyes are red from weariness, but, funny, my body isn't tired. I welcome this day with open arms, ready to face what lies ahead. Oh, yes, and Lord, thank you for allowing me this opportunity to come full circle. I know I couldn't have done it without you. I blow out the candles, and the scent of jasmine wafts through the air. I eagerly inhale the aroma and close my eyes. The fear is still there, but it is restrained for now, yet crouching in the wings, waiting for me.

I begin to recite Psalm 27: "*The Lord is my light and my salvation; whom shall I fear? The Lord is the strength of my life; of whom shall I be afraid?*" I turn out the lights, comforted by the knowledge that I have nothing to fear. I have no reason to be afraid. I just have to live.

Samantha Ducloux

The Zebra

After two decades writing around the edges of other professional activities that included teacher, counselor, and curriculum developer, Samantha Ducloux is currently treating herself to more time with this passion. Her publications include juvenile fiction and adult nonfiction for both the popular and education markets.

When not writing, she divides her time between building relationships with her new husband and six adult stepchildren and their families; enjoying her own three adult children; nurturing friendships; ballroom dancing; and playing with her dog, cat, and horse. She watches constantly for zebras.

MY NEW LIFE MIGHT HAVE STARTED WITH A ZEBRA. When she pranced off the circus truck to join the parade of animals walking to Portland's coliseum, the perfect symmetry of her black and white stripes made my breath catch. She passed so close that I could see

35

the individual bands of color encircling her body and extending up through her mane, each line as precise as if it had been drawn using an artist's straightedge. To me, the white stripes represented the traditionally feminine traits of submission and supportiveness that I'd been taught to emulate. They were beautiful. But those black stripes, stripes of independence and aggression, in combination with the white, were what gave the animal her unique sense of harmony and balance.

I fell in love with her. I wasn't yet thinking about how one-sided and discordant my own life was. But an unconscious part of me knew, "I want to be white and black too."

"You did an amazing thing," my daughter said yesterday, two decades after the zebra sighting. "You weren't very strong and you still saved our family. Because of you I know that somewhere within me, maybe just in my big left toe, I have enough strength to leave my relationship too. How did you do it?"

How did I? Even at that time, when I was still a young mom trying to appease an unappeasable man, I, like my daughter, must have had strength in my left toe. Women have historically been strong. Not necessarily strong as in bench pressing two hundred pounds or flexing pecs, but strong as in being emotionally able to do hard things. In the American West of the late 1800s and early 1900s some women even established their own homesteads, while back East others led social reform in critical areas like child labor. Clearly, strength is a good thing.

But if I had strength, I hid it well. I grew up unsure if it was desirable to be a strong woman. With a first-edition copy of the proto-feminist book *The Feminine Mystique* in one hand and *Fascinating Womanhood*, a self-help book for successfully subjugating yourself to men, in the other, I was thoroughly confused about the kind of person I wanted to be. Or, to be more accurate, the kind of person I should be. For a while, when I was in college in the mid-sixties, I tried to figure it out. Then I got married, started raising a family, and lost myself in the challenges that followed. Unconscious became the way to get through life.

Fortunately for my children and me, the zebra's lesson, coming fifteen years into an oppressive marriage, took hold anyway. Despite my confusion and feelings of helplessness, I embarked on a journey that would eventually lead to the discovery of my strength. Or perhaps the development of it. The next stop on that journey involved a horse.

I had reluctantly moved with my husband to 600-square-foot shack on ten acres in the hills just outside Portland. I hadn't wanted to leave our comfortable suburban house at the end of a cul-de-sac in a well-kept residential neighborhood ten minutes from downtown. My daughter, then entering fifth grade and as social as the stereotypic preteenager, had a good friend across the street and another just a block away. My older son was scheduled to start second grade at the close-by elementary school with an excellent teacher and a circle of playmates that had been together since preschool. My four-year-old son could peddle his Big Wheel up the sidewalk past three houses to play with his best friend when he wasn't at his cooperative play school. I didn't want to disrupt their busy, happy lives. Not to mention mine, as I was completing a contracted book and teaching part-time. But my husband said he was going, with or without the family. I didn't see that I had a choice.

Every time I drove up to the shack, I had to sit in the car for several minutes while I arranged a smile on my face. Grayed cedar shingles hung here and there from the exterior tar-papered walls. Inside, the children had to climb slats nailed against a wall as a ladder, to reach the unfinished attic where they slept. This place had actually housed another family once upon a time. But that had been a different era. Perhaps their children hadn't minded the absence of any bedrooms save the one their parents occupied. Nor the two-hole outhouse still standing across our driveway. I don't know how they had cooked and bathed. We used a porta-potty and plugged an electric frying pan into our one electric outlet, not just to make dinner, but to heat water from a fifty-gallon drum so we could wash dishes and hands. The plan was to live in what I euphemistically called our cabin while we, ourselves, added a kitchen and bathroom to it, then built an energy-efficient house farther up the hill. We'd put in a large garden too, and create a self-sufficient lifestyle. All this with no mortgage.

The dream of a self-sufficient lifestyle in the 1980s was laudable. We would all learn a bevy of skills, protect the environment, and create financial security for ourselves. But it was my husband's dream, not mine. And not the children's. I figured I was one of our nonrenewable resources and I was being completely used up. Still, I might have been able to share in his vision if we had not all had to endure his constant criticism and his vehement disregard for any of our interests at variance with his. This, when we were all working so hard and doing our very best to please him.

Then, one serendipitous day a year after we moved to the farm, friends asked if we could pasture their pony. Suddenly I could live a dream of my own! All my life I had wanted a horse. By the time I was eight I had read every horse book in the library and often walked alone to the neighborhood grocery store, where I would sit on the mechanical horse that required a dime to move, and imagine myself galloping across fields on a golden palomino. Now I had a real live palomino, half Arab and half Welsh, in my backyard. I rode him every day for months.

When the pony proved dangerous to my daughter, deliberately wiping her off his back with the branch of a convenient tree, I returned him to our friends and bought my first horse, Magic. She was a velvety bay mare with a white star and two white socks, and a lovely way of tickling my cheek with the stiff whiskers of her muzzle. My husband hadn't minded keeping our friends' pony, but he very much minded my having my own horse. We argued about it daily, although I provided all the care and shots, mended all the fences, and dug the drain fields through the pasture with a friend's help, not his.

I knew he was resentful of my using time and money this way, but from the day we had gotten married he'd lived by the principle that anything not his own idea was without merit. I was tired of it. I was now teaching full-time to pay the bills, as well as working many hours with him on the new house and doing all the chauffeuring to the children's extracurricular activities like soccer and music lessons, which he considered a waste of time. When I rode Magic along our maple-lined country road, I felt a sense of well-being completely new to me.

I didn't actually think about how, for the first time in eighteen years of marriage, I was standing up for something I personally wanted. I simply kept Magic. I might not be developing black stripes yet, but at least I was working on gray splotches as I moved toward a balance between meeting others' needs and meeting my own. My inner voice was cheering, "Go, girl!"

A friendship with a remarkable woman, Lorene, made my journey toward harmony and balance a conscious one. She was both the supportive wife and talented homemaker I'd been taught women should be, and a bright, articulate, delightful person in her own right. I knew other women who personified the ideal wife and homemaker. And I knew women who were interesting, active people. But I had not met anyone like Lorene, so beautifully both. Or one who seemed to so completely understand, accept, and approve of me just as I was. I had taught high school students units on heroes and heroines for years and never stopped to think who my role models were until the moment I realized, "I want to be like Lorene."

It was going to be difficult to be like her. She was seventy, I was forty-four. She drove a new Mercedes SL 150, I drove an old Chevrolet Cavalier. And she radiated a sense of deep confidence and contentment that translated into a quiet presence of strength, whereas I hunched my shoulders around my growing depression and must have exuded sadness and despair.

I used to think I borrowed the strength from Lorene to move forward out of my depression. Now I know she helped me find more of my own strength. With her immense wisdom and compassion, she reached out to me in ways that gave me the courage to begin talking about the darkness of my inner life and my marriage. She never belittled me for my tears or my negative feelings, two things I was absolutely not allowed in my marriage and grew too ashamed of to share with other friends. Rather, she asked gentle questions and expressed such a profound concern for the children and me that I opened up to her. Without ever actually criticizing my husband, she helped me see that he was a tyrant to his family, though he was affable and helpful to the rest of the world. And she modeled a loving relationship with her husband wherein they aired differences of opinion with immense respect for each other, as well as genuine affection. I literally cried sometimes just watching them and realizing that a life so different from mine existed.

Once I started talking to Lorene and other friends, and became acutely aware of the extent of my, and my children's, depression, I thought for the first time about a separation. Despite several rounds of family counseling over the course of our marriage, nothing had changed the way my husband treated us. My children and I needed a life away from constant criticism of both what we thought and what we did, as well as the opportunity to pursue our own interests and dreams. I had a stable job, so I had the money. I was building a network of close friends, so I had the support. Some of my gray splotches were getting sort of long and thin. But months passed. Arguments at home escalated. Still I couldn't actually make the break.

I turned to self-help books, reading everything I could find from *Codependent No More* to *Circle of Stones* to *The Blade and the Chalice*. In my journal, which had always been more a record of events than a chronicle of my heart, I began to write not just what I thought, but how I felt. Ideas and emotions sorted and resorted themselves.

My daughter, now sixteen, tired of crying every night, asked if she could live with a friend. I gave her my blessing. My fourteen-year-old son sobbed every afternoon down on the basement rug, beyond any comfort I could offer. My eleven-year-old son said, "Don't worry, Mom, I can forget anything. Sometimes it takes a week, but I can do it." And he went to his room to lie face down on the bed and forget another encounter with his father. I folded my arms over my broken heart, grimaced at my puny gray stripes, and stayed a little longer.

Would my journey end right here, on ten acres, with a husband who could find forty-five things I had done wrong in any given twenty minutes, and three miserable children? What would it take to buck the internalized teachings of my family, my church, and society as I experienced it?

I sought professional help. I needed deprogramming, I said. I needed to believe it was OK to be strong. I'd gladly face the pain of unconscious hurts and fears to free myself of their power and be able to take positive action in my life.

One night my husband got angry with my younger son and pushed him into some kitchen cabinets. Finally I'd had enough. I asked him to leave and he refused. So I called a friend who said the children and I could stay with her. I packed two suitcases for me and one each for my children, loaded everything into my Cavalier, and crunched down our long gravel driveway toward a new life. It had been six months since I'd thought of leaving, but my stripes were growing darker with each bend in the road.

By that time, I knew that the separation would be just one of many milestones on my journey. It takes two to have a bad relationship and I couldn't blame just my husband for our problems. I had a lot of changing to do too. A decade later I'm still on the journey. I don't have Lorene's quiet confidence yet, but I have left depression behind. I've settled into a happy second marriage. I have a new horse, a chestnut Arab mare, very comfortable with having strong opinions of her own. And yesterday, when I looked in the mirror, I thought I caught a glimpse of a zebra.

Mary Ann Baker

Clothes Do the Adventurer Make

Mary Ann Baker is a graduate of NYU's Department of Dramatic Art. As an aspiring actress she chose the stage name Fawn Bliss. In 1957, at her first audition for an off-Broadway production, when the producer asked her name and she replied "Fawn Bliss," the middle-aged woman removed her glasses, did a slow-take up, and said, "Now really, dear!"

After graduation, her first job was in a large New York City high school, teaching speech and theater, followed by marriage, two sons, a daughter, and a Marjorie Morningstar life in New Rochelle, New York.

After obtaining a graduate degree in education, she taught for fifteen years. From 1981 to 1991 Mary Ann worked in the Caribbean with her husband and three children rebuilding Anne Kristine, *the world's oldest sailing ship, and teaching teenagers and adults to sail a traditionally rigged ninety-five-foot schooner. They documented this experience for a film lecture, which they present from Maine to California. After losing their beloved ship in 1991's* The Perfect Storm, *Mary Ann started writing. From the quiet of her rural home she found inspiration for poetry and stories. She also ran marathons and biked 300 miles from Boston to New York in four days to raise money for AIDS research.*

Her poetry has been published in The Berkshire Review, *stories in* Chrone *magazine, essays and investigative journalism in* The Women's Times, *and commentaries aired on local National Public Radio stations. She is currently facing the largest challenge of her life, with rougher seas than any hurricane: lung cancer. But with her husband/navigator at her side, the love of family and friends, living in her daughter and son-in-law's home during treatment, and playing with three delightful and funny young grandchildren, she's sure to brave the elements and reach the calm at the end of this imperfect storm.*

I'VE CLIMBED THE HIGHEST HEIGHTS, SAILED THE bluest oceans, ridden the swiftest horses, kayaked the whitest rivers, marathoned on foot and pedal. And for what? The challenge? The adventure? The thrill of the dare? No! No! No! I did it all for the costumes, the outfits, the "look."

Nothing sweaty or sporty had ever entered my citified life until I met Norman. I was a fashionable young New York woman. He was a rugged, worldly outdoorsman. After we'd been dating awhile, he invited me to join him on a winter skiing holiday in Canada. I accepted, neglecting to inform him that everything I knew about skiing I had gleaned from a travel agency's ski vacation poster I'd seen on the subway. For weeks, I'd stare at this poster, which was between the handsome Marlboro Man and December's Miss Subway, a pretty blond secretary from Brooklyn, and fantasize about the attractive couple in the travel ad. He was blond (like Norman); she was brunette (like me), and both wore great looking, colorful ski outfits. I, too, wanted to stand atop a mountain with my fair-haired skier.

My reflection in the dressing room mirror at Ohrbach's Department Store on Thirty-fourth Street was both outdoorsy and sexy. The tight black nylon ski pants were topped by a snow-white, cable-knit Norwegian sweater with reindeer that pranced across the small hills of my bosom. I completed the look with a camel-hair cape, admittedly not designed for skiing, but which I thought gave dramatic completion to my costume. I now had the proper ski clothes and the Nordic-looking man. I felt quite ready for the snow-covered mountain.

In Canada, in full regalia, I rode up the Mt. Tremblant chair lift and disembarked. New skis pointing downhill, standing ramrod straight, poles raised high, I was soon airborne. Over the ridges and down the mountain I went, camel-hair cape billowing in the wind, until I miraculously slowed to a stop at the base without damage to my body or to the outfit. Norman soon was at my side. When he commented on my unusual nonbending style, I admitted that this was my first time on skis. Lessons followed. Forty years later, I still have the camel-hair cape and the blond ski instructor.

Not too long after my dramatic descent of Mt. Tremblant, Norman and I got married, and on our honeymoon I unexpectedly became a mountain climber. Norman had wanted to climb the Matterhorn, so we went to Zermatt, the storybook Swiss town at the base of this very high, craggy mountain. When the snows melt, Zermatt, with its horse-drawn carriages, thatch-roofed chalets, lederhosen, dirndl skirts, and bells and yodels, becomes a mecca for climbers.

Norman and I went shopping for his mountaineering gear. I, with no intention of doing anything more than walking the trails, couldn't resist trying on the tan corduroy knickers, the heavy, blue-with-white-snowflakes woolen knee socks, the hand-knit-in-Zermatt white woolen sweater with decorative silver front snaps, and the natural-sheep-fiber climbing mittens.

The next day, in my new outfit, I escorted Norman to the base of the Riffelhorn, not so high as the Matterhorn, but still a very high mountain at about 10,000 feet. There we rendezvoused with Norman's Swiss guide, Norbi Reiner.

I was going to watch them set off for the top and then take a leisurely stroll back to the village. Norbi started to attach a rope to me. I tried to tell him that I was not a climber, that the clothes were just pretend, that I was scared to death of heights, that I never even took the elevator to the top of the Empire State Building.

"Oh," he smiled broadly, "Empire Building, King Kong, he big ape, and you big strong woman in correct clothes. You climb!"

And so in my authentic alpining outfit, I found the minuscule cracks and the handholds and footholds, and got belayed and cajoled to the summit of the Riffelhorn.

On top, the three of us sat on a ridge overlooking glaciers with their slow-moving specks of animals. In the distance, the cloud curtain opened and for some minutes we could see the scraggy peak of the Matterhorn. We talked. Norbi wanted to know about America. Did we think the young John Kennedy could win over Richard Nixon? What kind of music did we listen to? Over cheese sandwiches and oranges, we exchanged ideas. And then Norbi guided us safely down the mountain.

Later on our honeymoon, Norman went on to conquer the Matterhorn. My one ascent of the Rifflehorn was enough to lend authenticity to my outfit. I still have the blue sweater and a photo Norman took of my behind in the tan corduroy knickers as he followed me up the Rifflehorn.

Back in the states Norman, an avid horseman, wanted me as a riding partner. I told him that the only thing I rode was the subway.

He started leaving his glossy *Horse and Rider* magazines lying around the apartment, casually opened to pictures of jodhpurs with suede inserts; sexy, shiny leather boots; and black velvet hats like Elizabeth Taylor wore in *National Velvet* with Mickey Rooney.

"OK," I finally said, and went with him to Miller's Equestrian Emporium on Twenty-third Street, where I chose a smart-looking riding costume. When I stepped from the dressing room and made my appearance, Norm was talking horse talk with Mr. Miller, the store's owner. I smilingly approached them and did a model pose, hand on hip, one foot pointed, then a half turn.

"This is swell," I said. "I'll take it."

Norm happily replied, " You look great, like you've been riding for years, but it's important to try out the seat and fit of the jodhpurs before we buy." He directed me to climb onto a saddle mounted on a stand." I did, feeling like the essence of equestrian glamour, that is, until Norm sidled near and whispered in my ear, "Get off. You're facing the horse's tail." In a careful undertone, he continued, "Walk around and get on from the other side." I did as he said and was looking at the horse's rear again. Nonplussed I dismounted again. Before I could start another go-round, Norman took my arm and guided me back to the dressing room.

Of course we bought the outfit. I soon learned how to walk, trot, and canter a horse. And I always make sure I have the horse's ears in front when I mount.

Today, I live in a western Massachusetts hill town and spend most of my time in the outdoors. My closet bulges with stylish running, skiing, walking, hiking, biking, and riding tops, bottoms, and footwear. I thought my sporting mishap days were over until I took an unexpected swim down the Deerfield River.

For years I had wanted to try fly-fishing. In early spring, driving along Route 9, I'd see the occasional solitary figure standing in the rapids of the west branch of the Westfield River. Again, the outfit. Thigh-high boots, the vest with a myriad of small pockets, the floppy hat with the license pinned to it. It became my dream to someday stand as they did in the sparkling white water.

This was realized when a friend asked if I'd like to go fly-fishing with her. My large feet could fit her husband's boots. She'd bring his rod. Norman had the fishing vest. I had the hat. On a Tuesday in mid-July we met at six in the morning in a parking lot. The air was still, the sky a Santa Fe blue with puffy white clouds.

"A perfect fly-fishing day," Stephanie said as she handed me her husband's outfit. After stepping into the boots, looping their loops around my belt, donning the vest, and pinning the license onto my hat, I was looking, I thought, quite nifty. Stephanie taught me about flies and rods and casting and told me things like, "It's best to stay close to the bank of the river" and "We only have a few hours to fish before they open the dam."

Soon we were ready for the Deerfield. A red-tailed hawk swooped overhead, back and forth, through the winding pass. It was a beautiful, peaceful spot.

Upstream from Stephanie, I had started at the river's edge and slowly picked my way around and over the mossy, slippery stones until I was casting off in the middle of the river. Focused on the delicate line and the white-winged tiny fly I'd carefully tied to it, I was rhythmically reeling in and out. A tug on the line interrupted my Zen state. I reeled in too fast and lost the fish but not my fly. About to cast off again, I realized the water that had been up to my knees was now reaching my thighs, and what sounded like a train was coming down on me. The dam had opened! The rising, rapid water knocked me over. Swimming with the current, I got downstream, grabbed Stephanie's outstretched hand and scrambled ashore.

Stephanie took a picture of me emptying the river from the thigh-high boots. I stripped out of my wet clothes and put on a poncho that

Stephanie had in the trunk of her car. It provided sticky coverage to my bare, wet body. By now it was noon and time for lunch at a nearby inn. The harried waitress who served us took slight notice of my dining costume. That afternoon a Day-Glo–green, plastic poncho was my fashion statement.

You'd suppose, by now, I've done it all. What's left? Well, the latest issue of Norman's *Air and Space* magazine just arrived, and those astronaut costumes—hmmm!

Sandy Kay Bryant

Cooking with Feeling: The Art of Woodstove Cooking

Sandy Kay Bryant grew up in Malaysia, where her parents were Lutheran missionaries. She lives in Chelan, Washington, in a log home she and her husband built themselves. Sandy has published one book, about the experience referred to in her essay, of living on the shores of a remote mountain lake, titled Mountain Air: The Life of Gordon Stuart, Mountain Man of the North Cascades.

THERE WAS A TIME WHEN I KNEW THE TEMPERATURE of an oven by how long I could hold my hand inside it. It wasn't as scientifically exact as equating a certain number of seconds to a certain number of degrees, but I could tell if the oven was hot enough to bake bread or too hot, likely to scorch the biscuits. At the time I was living in the Cascade Mountains on the shore of a remote lake, accessible only by hiking trail or floatplane. I did all my cooking and baking in a timeless old wood-burning cookstove owned by an equally timeless woodsman who employed me as caretaker.

That was ten years ago. Now I am married and live on a dirt road fifteen miles from the nearest small town. Once again I am baking in a wood-burning cookstove, but this time I succumbed to high-tech luxury and purchased an interior oven thermometer. After all, you can *drive* to this house. I thought I may as well go modern and save the hair on my forearms.

From cutting the wood to the act of turning the bread around in the oven because of hot spots, cooking on a woodstove is probably one of the most grounding activities I have ever learned. It teaches me to be mindful of what is around me. My awareness of sound and sensation is sharpened, letting the overworked sight rest a bit, relaxing into a more rounded and holistic experience of cooking.

When I am getting to know a new woodstove—as I did in this new home—I operate almost as though I am a blind woman. I go by sound and feel, running my hand across the stove half an inch or so above the surface to discover the hottest spot, listening for the changes in draft as I adjust the dampers. It took probably a good month to really become familiar with the cookstove I use now, but now that I know the stove, I work with it as with a friend.

I am sitting at the kitchen table in a room where black cast-iron frying pans hang in neat rows from the homemade log rafters. It is bread-baking day in my kitchen. Two whole-grain loaves are rising in the open warming oven above the range, steam curling around the loaf pans from the teakettle simmering below. On the back of the stove, navy beans and vegetables are cooking together slowly in a favorite enameled soup pot.

I move to the stove and check the fire. It is barely mulling along, and the oven is too cool right now for the bread that will be ready to go into it soon. I need to turn up the heat. Crouching next to the stove, I twist the stainless-steel bell dampers wide open, then swing open the firebox door and root through the nearby wood box for just the right sticks to throw in—medium-small, the kind that go on top of the kindling when you're building a fire. And white pine, not fir. "White pine burns like hay," my friend the woodsman used to say, scorning it. Yes, it does. Just the thing to turn up that oven. In a matter of minutes I can feel the increased intensity of the heat.

So many things go into regulating the heat of a woodstove oven and cooking surface: the type of wood, how dry it is, what size it is cut, the shapes into which it is split, the cleanliness of the stove and chimney, the damper settings. Round, unsplit lengths of fir—from the bigger limbs or smaller tops of trees—will keep a fire the longest. The same fir split into sticks about an inch thick will give you a fire hot enough for stir-frying.

The bread is ready to go into the oven now. I slash the arching tops of the loaves with a sharp knife and slide them in to bake. In ten or fifteen minutes I'll turn them around to keep them browning evenly. This oven has a hot spot in the right-rear corner.

One of the major differences between modern gas or electric stoves and wood cookstoves is that you use your ears a lot to know what's going on with a cookstove, whereas with modern stoves you're likely to use your eyes. I can tell how my fire is doing by its sound: the intensity of the crackling or the relative silence punctuated by the occasional pop, and all the stages in between. After those two years at the lake of cooking exclusively on a woodstove, my first visit to a "regular" kitchen left me feeling vaguely restless. What was it? I couldn't say for sure . . . and then I realized: I was missing the sound of the fire, and my restlessness came from the conviction that as quiet as things were, I surely needed to be jumping up and stoking it. The sound of the fire had become a companion to my time in the kitchen, a subconscious voice that I listened to ceaselessly. Only in its absence did I become completely aware of it.

◊◊◊

I can hear the navy-bean soup beginning to bubble more vigorously in its pot on the back of the stove. I slide the pot a little to the right—further from the firebox—and open the oven door to sneak a peek at the thermometer. Just as I suspected, things are also getting too hot for the good of the bread inside. I shut the dampers down and add larger chunks of slow-burning fir to cool things down. I'll keep an eye on it. If those measures still aren't enough, I can always open the oven damper and let some of that heat escape up the chimney.

Cooking on a woodstove is often perceived as difficult and tricky, but in reality it is just a matter of learning a different set of cues for the things you need to know. These days, I really have to focus myself when confronted with operating an electric or gas stove. I read the burner labels out loud—Right Front, Left Rear, Hot, Medium, Low, Off—turning the knobs with the caution of someone who expects electrocution.

My "burner adjustment" consists of sliding the pots around on the surface of the cookstove, or slipping a trivet underneath them. I have two old-fashioned Pennsylvania Dutch cast-iron trivets that I use all the time, and two steel racks that I use less frequently for the same purpose. One of those racks doubles as a toaster when I remove a circular stove lid and lay the slice of bread on the rack over the open fire. *That* toaster never breaks down.

Come to think of it, there seem to be several electrical kitchen appliances that I have never needed because I cook on a woodstove. A toaster is one. A Crock Pot is another. (A Dutch oven simmering its contents on the back of a woodstove is the original Crock Pot.) My wok fits perfectly into the hole created when one of the stove lids is removed, and it warms up quickly to the temperatures required for stir-frying. Since the cookstove surface is entirely flat, there is never a problem of a frying pan or griddle too large to fit on a burner. My pancake griddle is a fourteen-inch round slab of Vermont soapstone, well seasoned now from years of Sunday-morning pancake breakfasts.

Of course, there are drawbacks to cooking on a woodstove. It can seem like it will take longer to deliver that promised cup of tea to the neighbor who drops in if you are starting from a cold stove (though I bet if you timed it with an electric stove, a good clean woodstove stuffed with small sticks of fast-burning white pine might win the race). You do have to clean the chimney regularly—but when else do you get to see what's lately landed on your roof? And if you don't have an oven thermometer, your forearm may sometimes sport that curious hairless look that is so hard to explain to downtown cooks.

The bread is coming out of the oven now—brown loaves, fragrant and hot. I pick up a knife with the quiet awareness that now I am going to slice some bread for supper. I watch as the blade cuts through the tiny strands of gluten, and am conscious of the released smell of scented grain as I spread the steaming slices with butter and honey. I lift the pot from the back of the stove, open the lid, and dip a wooden ladle into the soup, filling a blue-willow soup plate. The kitchen fills with mingled aromas.

I have long had a certain philosophy in my life that whatever you do becomes a part of you. Doing things with awareness, experiencing times of serenity and happiness and harmony—somehow they get inside of you and become part of who you are and what people see in you, whether others have shared in those moments or not. If this is true, then perhaps the goodness of this homemade bread also comes not only from the fresh-ground flour and deep well water, but from the meditative enjoyment that I experience in cooking on a woodstove and tending fire. Everything contributes. It matters what I feel and notice: the silky dough beneath my hands, the grain and color of the wood as I feed it to the fire, the light of morning sun slanting through the window and making latticework shadows on the raisin bread recipe. These are healthy moments in the body of my life. My soul is nourished by these moments of timelessness just as a body is strengthened by wholesome food. If I had not absorbed them, my inner peace would be less.

I let the fire die down; my mind has gone quiet with it. Glowing embers make no sound at all. Before bedtime, I will find it cool enough to lay the morning's fire. Without a movement, I have turned my stove to Off.

Amy Carmickle

Sheets upon the Line

Amy Carmickle was born in eastern Oregon in 1960 into a large and colorful family. Her father, of Irish heritage, grew up in Boston and came west after World War II to attend Stanford University. He met her mother, a feisty Norwegian from a small town in Minnesota, on his journey. As family legend has it, Amy's mother, desirous of adventure and a life beyond the Midwest, ran away with her father not long after they met. Amy always found it easy to envision in her mother, even after age, sadness, and sickness had taken their toll, that excited girl who loved fun and would do a thing like take off in the middle of the night with a handsome man she had only just met.

Growing up, Amy remembers a good deal of laughter in her home. Creativity, ingenuity, individuality, and compassion were revered, and she hopes she has passed along to her sons, Joey and Josh, now young adults, many of the same values. Both her sons are currently college students.

Amy recently earned a Master of Arts degree in English and will teach creative writing at Portland State University in 2002. And she is, of course, writing, and learning as she goes along to write and live better and better—always striving toward that goal and always learning.

SOME DELICATE FIBER RAN BETWEEN MY MOTHER AND me, connecting us. A fine spider silk that vibrated gently as if touched by a breath or the tip of a finger, sending messages to be transcribed by the receiver. And so I knew, before the signs became evident, before the diagnosis was made, that she was dying—knew by the quivering of the thread.

I could not believe that death could ever take this woman, so bodily tough that she'd run barefoot outdoors in the icy wetness of a Portland winter, and coarse enough, when provoked, to outswear the roughest teenage boy on the block. There had been a time when I thought she would outlive me; or perhaps it was some secret, rather grim little wish that I might go first so that I would not have to exist without my mother, calling me every night, wanting to know all the details of my not-so-exciting life.

Her vast loneliness birthed a vast intrusiveness upon the life of her daughter, who endured it because this mother was the sort who, when you stopped by to visit and could not find her inside the house, might be found scratching around on the roof, at the age of seventy-six, perched there like some new species of bird, cleaning the eaves. And you knew just as well that you must stifle your first impulse, which was of course to yell, "For God's sake, Mother, get down from there! Aren't you afraid you're going to fall!" You realize you must leave her to the scraping of leaves and crud, because she was probably at her happiest up there doing that kind of thing (and if you were to have yelled, she would only have looked at you as if you were crazy or something, anyway).

Endured it because this was a woman who had lost her only son at his birth and forever grieved him—could never truly mend from the loss, yet set about fixing every cracked and broken thing about her, and worked hard to distract herself from her pain—mowing the sprawling lawn at the old farmhouse we lived in outside of Pendleton when I was a child, and sewing clothes for me and all six of my sisters.

Endured it because she taught me—daughter number five—to make tiny dolls out of hollyhocks. "See, look here," my mother told me, "the toothpick goes up through the center of the open flower, just like that. And then the closed bud you stick on top for the head and there, you have a pretty little doll with a beautiful open skirt."

She would not have thought to join the PTA or volunteer as a room mother when I sat behind a grade school desk and it seemed all the other mothers handed out cupcakes and fruit punch and I fantasized about having an ordinary mother who might do that sort of thing.

"I'd love to meet your mom sometime," my second-grade teacher said to me one day. I turned my head and said nothing. But a vision sprung to mind of my mother in the sunshine hanging sheets that she had just forced with her strong hands through the washer's slowly rotating wringer. And me, I am standing there impatient for the last clothespin to grasp that final bit of cloth because I have great plans to run through the long, cool corridors of sheets and feel them brush deliciously up against the August heat of my cheeks and whip across my naked arms, and nobody can see me running there (which is the most splendid thing of all). But my mother spies the quick girl's feet between clean sheets.

She does not yell, "Get out from there! You might pull them down or dirty them with your chubby just-made-mud-pies hands!" Instead, she calmly scoops the empty clothes basket up in her tanned arms and walks away, leaving the wild girl to run and giggle joyously through the maze of just-washed sheets upon the line.

This is why I did my best to ward off the disease of loneliness that preyed on her as relentlessly and mercilessly as the cancer, leaving me, in the end, unsure which one truly could claim credit for taking her life.

Unfounded fears and anxieties served both to insulate and confine her, as my mother had such a craving for life. Her growth was checked and desire reined in by paralyzing doubt—she, a victim unwillingly bound to familiar ground. No, second-grade teacher or ladies who gather to play cards in the afternoon at the senior center or who meet on the golf course or tennis courts or who roam through art galleries or take Carnival cruises, you will never meet my mother.

Waking from a dream a week after she died, I am sobbing in my dream and for real; the tears roll onto my pillow and I am shouting in my dream and for real; my voice shocks me out of sleep and dream, and what I am saying to my mother is, "I don't want you to be dead!" Me, willfully, emphatically, insisting like a child who fancifully might believe that just by wanting he can make it so.

"Your hand feels so cold, Mother," I said to her as she lay on the hospital bed the hospice delivered, which now sat in the living room in the house on Douglas Street that somehow stopped being her house once the cancer was diagnosed. I covered her more tightly with the blanket. Then, "Is that better; does that feel better?" And she looked at me and the tears in her eyes mirrored my own. "Are you in pain?" I said, "I don't want you to be in pain." But looking closer, it was fear I read there in her eyes. The brown, bitter morphine could not wipe away the fear, and I knew that she looked to me—had always looked to me—daughter number five, for comfort, for understanding, so I stifled my own fear and squeezed her hand and smiled at her. The message my eyes sent moved now down that secret thread that attached us, and the receiver transcribed. Then her face grew easy, innocent, like a child's. I kissed her on the forehead as she had kissed me when I was small and in need and it was her kiss that had made me easy. "I love you," I told her.

We never spoke those words "I love you," my mother and me. Its obviousness seemed to deem the statement foolishly redundant—but somehow now . . . just in case there had ever been any doubt . . . "I love you," she repeated.

"I have to go," I said, or maybe it was she who said it.

I heard from my sister that my mother let go after I left, went to that place to which people go between life and death, where no one or nothing is familiar anymore. And the early-morning call to officially announce her passing came, but I did not need to answer. I had already felt the pang as the fine thread detached. The inconsolable ache as I watched it float gracefully away.

◊ ◊ ◊

Self-sufficiency is, at best, an illusion. While we are taught from day one to strive toward some ideal state of independence, where all connections to others are optional and irrelevant to our ultimate survival, I contend that no such state exists, because as humans, it matters immensely to us, at some core and vital level, that we are not alone—that we matter to someone. Whether we live or die or hurt or cheer at the top of our lungs with glee, we need to know that someone out there cares about us. If not, we simply cease to fully be, somehow. We become dulled, flattened, our life experiences not wholly lived, because they have not been shared with another, and our perspectives turn singular, narrowed, skewed.

There have been times in my life when I've blurted to complete strangers some great joy or great heartache that I could not contain, so immediate was the need to share my emotion with another. I have also been on the receiving end of such encounters. Not so long ago, while I was jogging through a nearby neighborhood, an elderly woman getting her mail stopped me as I went by her house, and held me there by her mailbox with her talk. She chatted on for several moments about nothing consequential and I wondered what this lady—petite, meticulously kempt, but drawn-looking nonetheless beneath her neat arrangement of clothes and hair and makeup—I wondered what she wanted from me, just what type of revelation she was building to.

Eventually, her face clouded and her voice took on an edge as she told me that a year ago to the date, her son had died unexpectedly in his sleep—a young man, still, at thirty-eight. And she, after all these long months, could not believe he was gone. She brought his picture out to show me and I looked at him like I had known him my entire life, truly felt for a fleeting glint of time that perhaps I had.

She never spoke to me before that day, and though I've passed by her house since, she's not done more than wave briefly in recognition. She only had needed someone at that precise moment, on that very day, when memories overwhelmed her and became too much to bear alone. And I happened to be passing by. Perhaps she's even embarrassed or surprised by her behavior, letting down her guard like that, exposing such intimate feelings to a stranger. Don't be, I want to tell her. Self-sufficiency is an illusion, and for all the value we place on strength and standing on our own, we are still only humans, reaching out to each other to make sure we're not alone. We are, every one of us, needy like that.

Jeanne Faulkner

Full Cart

Jeanne Faulkner lives in Portland, Oregon, with her husband, four children, and father. She works as a nurse in the labor and delivery unit of a large regional medical center. She reads too much, exercises a little, and does quite a lot of grocery shopping. Other than chasing kids around town, she pursues a habit as a word junkie, writing stories, essays, and articles about birth and pregnancy, raising kids, aging parents, and breast cancer. She cooks a lot and entertains too often, thus the penchant for marketing. She works with her husband at rehabbing their nearly 100-year-old house and spends far too much time cleaning it up.

SOME PEOPLE NEED A DRAMATIC MOMENT TO SEE their life flash before their eyes. I just need to go to the grocery store. I had an epiphany in the checkout lane recently.

Just looking at my cart gives some people the jitters. The sheer quantity of products is astounding. Sometimes I have to use two carts.

That gives me the jitters. My cart reveals a lot about me and my life. For instance, at least twice a month, I end up buying the full spectrum of hygiene products—from incontinence to feminine to baby. It's not hard to spend over fifty dollars on this stuff. I've got the Huggies Supreme Care for the baby. I've got the Always ultratrim maxi-pads for the adolescent girls. I've got the Always extra long, super-sized, ultramaxi for the perimenopausal me. And then I've got the medium-size Depends pull-up pants for Grandpa. Sometimes, I also buy the little Depends liners when he's feeling frisky and wants to wear regular underwear. (There's an accompanying spectrum of laundry and cleaning supplies to go with that mood.) It occurs to me that I really ought to slip the garbageman a tip for having to deal with the end results of all these products.

A trip to the dairy case is equally comprehensive. We buy the whole line of dairy fat. We've got whole milk for the baby and the too-skinny preteen. We've got the 2 percent for the other kids, who just aren't going to drink that blue nonfat milk I buy for myself. I had just better not come home without some buttermilk for the old guy. He likes to drink it with a little pepper. He'll recount his funny story about the time he served some buttermilk to his Chinese interpreter in Taiwan, who spit the stuff out on the table. Boy, that's a good one. I've heard that story gallons of times.

Most important, I have to get the half-and-half because you can be sure that I'm not going to get through a day without my coffee. And then, of course, the butter for all the after-school cookie fests the girls have with their friends. I swear their arteries are going to clog before they finish puberty. My husband is always trying to get a little more protein in his life, so we buy him the low-fat, small-curd cottage cheese. Big curds are yucky. Ask anyone.

Grandpa is dedicated to adhesive products. We spend a fortune on glue of all kinds. My cart will, variably, have five-minute and fifteen-minute epoxy, hot-glue gun sticks (short and long), Elmer's regular and wood glues and, of course, rubber cement. You can't imagine how excited he was when he discovered a dial-up glue stick in last year's bag of school supplies. A new day dawned for him and we've been keeping him supplied ever since. You can do anything if you have the right adhesive.

How about pain control? Another soup-to-nuts situation. We've got the Infant concentrated ibuprofen drops and baby Tylenol. You don't want to be without that on Friday night at 10:00 P.M. when an ear infection hits. We've got Motrin liquid in the orange flavor, not grape, for the five-year-old who gets charley horses and growing pains at 3:00 A.M. We've got Advil gel caps for all those cramps and headaches we menstruators get. My runner husband is partial to the Costco brand of ibuprofen that he can get in the über-sized 5,000 pill bottle, 'cause that's a bargain, you know. And nothing is better than Bayer Aspirin. It's been good enough for the old guy for fifty years and he can't figure out why anyone would take anything else. Unless, of course, you've got something else, and then he'll take that too. When I got sent home from the hospital last year with a new baby and some Percocet, all we needed was a good dose of morphine and we'd have had the complete range of pain relief covered.

But what about the rest of the food groups? Just take, for example, the protein portion of the pyramid. We are a quasi-vegetarian (dairy, eggs, fish) family with a meat-and-potatoes grandpa. So our shopping cart looks a bit strange. We've got three boxes of extra-firm tofu and four boxes each of fake bacon, soy sausages, and soy hamburger patties. We've got two pounds of salmon for Sunday-night dinner. We've got two kinds of peanut butter, old-fashioned, natural-style chunky with the oil separated on the top, and creamy Jif because, apparently, I'm a "choosy" mother.

We can clean out the bean aisle. We've got vegetarian refried beans for burrito night, and black beans for homemade soup. Hormel chili with beans is the only good kind that comes in a can. And, by the way, you can pick that up right next to the corned beef hash, which makes an excellent breakfast and has ever since Grandpa was a boy, about the time that his mother discovered you could get canned goods in a market. Boy, that was a big day, and he'll tell you about it every time you ask him what he wants at the store.

We're always scared when he asks for dried, red beans in the same breath he uses to ask me if I've seen the pressure cooker. You know that's the best way to cook a bean. You don't have to do anything but add the water and a can of tomatoes and wait. Remarkably, I haven't been able to find the pressure cooker since the last time he tried this famous recipe—and I still haven't cleaned all the tomato off the ceiling.

I never feel more inept than when I go to the butcher section. I had never cooked a piece of meat in my life until the day Grandpa moved in with us. Fortunately, we had the good sense and foresight to know that it would be a lot easier to learn to cook a pork chop than to turn the old guy into a vegetarian. However, I had no idea how much there is to learn about meat. And why is it that butchers are so eager to teach you all the ins and outs of a lamb roast when they hear you are a vegetarian? It's like you are a meat virgin and they want to be the first to initiate you into the joy of steak.

I recently made the mistake of asking the butcher for a roast. Who knew that there are at least a hundred types of roasts? "Could you be more specific, please?" he asked.

"Well, I don't know. How about a ten-dollar beef one?"

"A ten-dollar beef one? Excuse me, what cut? Shoulder? Rump? Rib?"

Asshole. "Sorry, I don't really know. I'm buying this for an old man and I really don't know much about it."

"You're a vegetarian, aren't you. Is this your first time?"

Oh shit, here we go. "Listen, I've got two kids in this cart who have their hands on a lot of messy stuff that they are just itching to throw. I'll trust your judgment. You just pick out a ten-dollar beef one and nobody will have to clean up. OK?"

"Fine, ma'am, but next time you might want to come in with a little more information."

And a stun gun, buddy. Just wrap up the meat. "Yes, I'll just do that."

I'm so much happier when I get to the produce section. I can dole out the plastic bags and turn the kids loose. Each one returns with a good supply of fruit or veggies of the week, and I can concentrate on the gross stuff. They pick out the apples, oranges, broccoli, and iceberg lettuce. I select the onions, foreign mushrooms, sprouts, and arugula. One of them is assigned to get Grandpa's cabbage. There's nothing better than fried-cabbage stew. There was that time when Grandma made cabbage stew for him when he worked the night shift at the factory and he'd eat a whole pot full of that stuff for breakfast when he got home. If I keep working at it, I might just figure that recipe out. I haven't gotten it right yet, but that doesn't keep him from bugging me.

I still feel a twinge of guilt when we buy grapes, green, not red. I've never gotten over the grape boycott of the '60s and '70s. We prefer a local Hood River apple if we can get it, as opposed to a Chilean Gala. We like to support our economy.

As a treat in the spring, we trundle over to the garden section of our grocery megastore. We each pick out a seed package to plant in this year's vegetable garden.

My husband supervises the flower selection: an assortment of stock, snapdragons, Shasta daisies, and, of course, sweet peas. There's no prettier flower than a sweet pea and none easier to grow. Grandpa will tell you that every time we plant the garden. He just doesn't remember that it's too cold here to get a good sweet pea going in March. Lord knows, we've killed plenty of them. We plant them anyway and he tells the story. Good enough.

He'll also tell you that you don't need to grow any vegetable in your garden other than corn. Golden Bantam corn, that's the best kind. Why, he's been growing that kind of corn all his life and it's better than any other kind of corn you can grow. It's sweeter, more delicious, and, by God, just better. You can buy all those other veggies in the store. I guess there's not much merit in mentioning that you can buy corn in the store too. But not Golden Bantam corn. The rest is just down-stream corn or city corn or something. Just for good measure, you bet-ter plant some tomatoes though. A nice Early Girl or Big Boy, that's all you need. And don't plant too many, you don't want that. No sir, there's nothing better than a nice warm, sun-ripened tomato with a little salt and pepper. You don't need anything else if you've got that. On this one subject, we are in agreement.

When it's time to check out, I don't look for the shortest line. Oh no, that's not the way a big-game shopper does it. No, the shortest line is for all those cute little gals with their handbaskets. If you have two baskets, like me, you look for the checker who shows the least fear. You've got to look them in the eye and make sure they see what they're up against. If it looks like they're up to snuff, you take them on.

Now, our market hires a lot of its help from an organization that trains the developmentally and mentally disabled. Well, bless their hearts, they do a fine job, but they just don't need to take on a huge endeavor like my order. Just bagging an order of this magnitude could knock them out of the game. I feel a little disabled myself when it comes to putting all this stuff away.

Unlike many, I'm not afraid of the candy-filled display next to the checker. I just figure that the Einsteins who designed the checkout aisle this way deserve it if my kids ingest the whole box of Snickers bars while I unload. I'm too distracted to stop them. And if I'm about to drop a big wad of cash in their store, well, they can just eat the profits if my kids eat the candy. That'll teach them.

Kids can impart quite a lot of stored-up wisdom in the checkout line. One day my then three-year-old daughter spoke up. "Hey, Mom, guess what?"

"Hmm? What?"

"Mom, *china* and *vagina* rhyme together."

Believe me, she said this loud enough that people were laughing all the way back to frozen foods. The old biddy behind me with the lemon-puckered lips scowled at me when I confirmed, "Well, they do, you know."

As the checker heaves a sigh and totals up the bill, I realize just what I've got here. My epiphany reveals itself to me as the total is read out in hushed tones, as if the number, read aloud, might shock me. I realize that what I've got here is a two-basket life, full of everything and more of some things than most can handle. I've got life's abundance, all double bagged, in paper, not plastic. There isn't anything else I need. I've got it all and I don't even shop with a list. Just load up the bags, buddy, and help me out to the car. I'll take it from there.

Kianga Jinaki Hanif

Do We Really Need to Know?

Kianga Jinaki Hanif is forty-three, a native of Baltimore, Maryland, and a graduate of Morgan State University. She is the mother of three sons, Nazim, Abasi, and Elijah, and one daughter, Ayize. She pays the bills by being a cloth-doll maker, quilter, storyteller, teacher, writer, and massage therapist.

Kianga's artwork has been shown throughout south Florida (and a few other places). She is also the owner of Talking Hands Therapeutic Massage Studio. Kianga has resided in Riviera Beach, Florida, for the past fifteen years.

THE OTHER DAY WHILE I WAS OUT RUNNING ERRANDS, a little girl walked up to me and said, "Excuse me, Miss, but what does your shirt mean?" I was wearing a T-shirt with a picture of Curious George lying spread eagle at the foot of an ether bottle.

I replied, " It means that there is some information that is not worth knowing."

Now don't get me wrong. As a writer and storyteller, I'm an information collector myself. I've forgotten more information than some people will obtain in a lifetime. I understand intimately that knowledge is power. Some of you may read this and say this is just a classic case of the pot calling the kettle "just another pot," but do we really need to know the intimate details of our neighbor's coworker's relationship with her husband?

I've reached the point in my life where I just tell people, "I really don't wanna know that," and walk away. And all those "I bet you'll be shocked by this" talk shows, I refuse to watch, and I stop other people when they want to tell me what they saw.

Things we once held personal, confidential, and even sacred are now fodder for public consumption. "People just don't have any shame anymore!" Joy, an elderly friend of mine, shared once as we discussed the current all-u-can-eat information-diet phenomenon.

Sometimes I wish I had a sign with the word "Information" circled in red with a bar going through it that I could hold up whenever I am about to be assaulted by information I'd rather not have. I'm convinced that part of the reason we can't remember important stuff, like turning the iron off or where we put the car keys, is that our minds are so full of unnecessary information that the important stuff can't get through.

Even the technology that we use to keep track of our exorbitant amount of information can reach its limit. Yesterday while trying to retrieve my e-mail, a message came up on the screen that said the computer was out of memory. "How could that be?" I thought. My computer functions as a glorified typewriter that, unlike my mind, saves everything I type into it for me to either retrieve or never retrieve again. It had reached its limit of information accumulation and needed me to eliminate some so it could receive more. A lesson that people should take note of, I thought.

In this age of information, anybody can find out almost everything about you by just pressing a few keys or numbers. Walking by the TV recently, I noticed a commercial for a service to help you "find anybody you want." All you had to do was dial 1-800-I WANNA KNOW. The first thought that popped into my mind was, But what if the person doesn't want you to find them?

Isn't it time we say enough already? Let's return some things to the personal, the sacred. When presented with the opportunity to tell all, take No out of the mental attic, dust it off, and give Yes a much needed rest.

A dear friend of mine doesn't have a radio in her car because she says, "That's just too much noise pollution in such a small space." When she made that statement a few years ago, I thought she was making an extreme decision. Now, I understand exactly where she was coming from. Like my friend's car, our minds are subjected to too much information for such a small space. The space I'm talking about is our lives.

Hopefully we are beginning to realize that it's time to stop living our lives like Curious George, and that some things really are none of our business.

Mary Wentworth

Orange Juice

Born just months before the 1929 stock market crash, Mary Wentworth grew up in a large family in a well-known Maine resort area, made more famous in the 1980s by the first Bush presidency. Shortly after World War II, she was accepted as a scholarship student at Smith College in Massachusetts.

After graduation in 1950, Mary taught school in New York state and then worked as a code breaker and translator at a top-secret Washington agency, where she encountered job discrimination because she was female. After her marriage in 1952, she lived in Philadelphia, becoming a full-time homemaker. As a stay-at-home wife with six children and a bread-winner husband, the marriage typified those of the period. After being drawn into political activism by the black-power and antiwar movements of the 1960s, Mary became a leader in the women's liberation movement.

In 1973, after a divorce, Mary relocated to Amherst, Massachusetts, and became involved in tenant organizing, stopping nuclear power, and supporting labor strikes. She continued to work on women's issues; amid political tours abroad, she became an advocate for low-income women and a Democratic candidate for the U.S. Congress.

Mary has written newspaper articles and columns, and given numerous radio and television interviews, lectures, and slide shows. Now retired, she remains active in local politics, offers on-air commentary on national and international events, and is working on completing a political autobiography.

RAYS OF THE LATE-WINTER SUN BRIGHTENED THE kitchen of the Victorian twin that my husband and I had purchased in the Germantown section of Philadelphia the previous December. We had actually had to cheat a bit to get the GI mortgage, because our projected income for 1956 had not met the bank's guidelines. Even with penny-pinching, we had a tough time covering basic living expenses.

This particular Monday morning I was supervising our two young daughters, ages twenty-two months and ten months, as they ate breakfast. My husband was making final preparations to get off to his job as assistant headmaster at a private school. An insomniac, Alex arose from wherever he had last attempted to sleep—this morning it was the sofa—driven by nervous tension. Tall, already nearly bald at twenty-nine, he moved rapidly through the sparsely furnished rooms. He was looking for his tie clip, annoyed that I did not know where he had put it.

Breakfast had brought to mind a situation that was beginning to concern me. On our Thursday-evening trips to the supermarket, we purchased a week's supply of orange juice for the family. Lately, this supply was depleted by Monday or Tuesday because my husband had fallen into the habit of drinking juice while watching evening television. Our two children were no longer receiving their daily allowance of Vitamin C two or three days out of the week.

"We're low on juice again," I said, spooning cereal into the baby's open mouth. He paused in the doorway, fastening his tie clip, and then stepped to the counter for a last gulp of coffee.

"Should we buy more?" I asked, turning to look at him as he put his cup in the sink. "We'd have to cut something else off the list." He made no reply as he headed out of the kitchen.

I called after him, "Could you find something else to drink?" In a moment or two, he reappeared, overcoat on, briefcase in one hand, car keys in the other.

He paused long enough to say in a flat tone of voice, "As long as you buy orange juice, Mary, I'm going to drink it."

I sat, baffled, as the heavy oak door closed behind him. Watching my daughters try to feed each other their pieces of toast, I repeated his response over and over in my mind, trying to twist his square peg of a response into one of my round-holed options for solving the problem. There didn't seem to be a fit. I puzzled over the phrase "as long as you buy." What did he mean by that? I had viewed our shopping trips as a joint venture, a sharing in deciding how to parcel out the one expenditure where we had some choices. Just because I went with a list of supplies that needed replenishing, jotted down as the week progressed, did this make it "my" buying trip? Hadn't he approved of the selections that went into the grocery cart? Wasn't he the one, after all, who pulled the cans of orange juice from the Food Fair freezer?

I lifted the baby out of her jumper chair and took the toddler by the hand for the climb up the stairs. I thought about the shopping trips and what they meant to me. For one thing, they offered a chance to get out of the house. Even with the two little ones along, they were a welcome change from the confinement of my daily routine. They also represented, I had thought, a degree of success in achieving the togetherness that the social arbiters of the day had decreed to be the hallmark of happy families. Did my husband's words "you buy" mean that I had failed?

Drawing a warm bath for the children, I felt the chill of loneliness settling in. Judging by his response, my attempts to deepen the companionship of our courtship days had been thwarted once again. I felt keenly my dependency on him to fill my needs for closeness and intimacy. Since our marriage, we had moved back and forth across the city. The moves occurred too quickly for mere acquaintance to be welded into lasting friendship. His mother and grandmother, both widows with distinct needs of their own, were hardly the ones a young mother could turn to for emotional support, and I had not yet gotten to know other mothers on our block.

As I placed the children, squiggling with anticipation, in the oversized, claw-foot tub, I turned my mind to the last phrase of my husband's statement. If I were to be solely responsible for buying, how could I plan with this kind of uncertainty? How much orange juice would he drink? Could he possibly have meant that he had no qualms about consuming our daughters' share as well as mine? Surely that was not his intention. Didn't he tell me that he loved me? Didn't he bring me breakfast in bed on Sunday mornings to let me know how much he cared?

My conscious thought jumped instinctively away from the answers to these questions in the same way my finger did if I touched the hot iron when I was pressing his shirts. I realized that my husband had inadvertently revealed himself to me. But my mind could not wrap itself around the import of his reply. Was it because I just could not bear alone the pain of the truth?

That evening, fussy children underfoot, I was making the final preparations for our evening meal. My husband stepped into the kitchen, home from his day at school. Our toddler shouted, "Daddy!" pointing her index finger in his direction. With a brief "How'r you?"

and a quick kiss, he emitted a sigh and, with shoulders slumping, disappeared toward the living room, evening paper in hand.

Later, his dinner eaten, he jumped up, before I had finished my dessert, to clear the table and wash the dishes, a task he had faithfully performed for his mother and now for me. Upstairs, I got the children into their nighties and, after the nightly ritual of picture books, tucked them into bed. As I went back into our bedroom to collect their clothes for the laundry basket, I discerned familiar sounds—the opening and closing of the refrigerator door, the running water, the spoon clinking against the side of the metal pitcher. My husband was preparing his evening's refreshment.

$$\emptyset \emptyset \emptyset$$

As long as you buy orange juice, Mary, I'm going to drink it. In one terse statement, he had served notice to me that not only would he not be involved in making a decision but that he had no qualms about sabotaging mine. Later in my life I learned that my husband's behavior has a name: emotional abuse. Most of us are familiar, if not through personal experience then through films, plays, and books, with the loud and angry name-calling, threats, and accusations that often accompany physical violence. But other manifestations, typical of my experience, can be more subtle. We know now that although emotional abuse always goes hand in hand with physical violence, it can also walk on its own two legs. Unlike physical assault, it leaves no telltale marks on the body's exterior, but batters and bruises the inner being. In fact, it is the emotionally abusive message, telegraphed to the victim via physical force, that inflicts more damage than the blackened eye or broken arm.

Like others in similar situations, I was confused by my husband's behavior because declarations of love and what appeared to be caring ministrations were sprinkled throughout the relationship, keeping me off balance by holding out the hope that perhaps we were growing closer after all. If only I had had the benefits then of the women's movement that came along in the late sixties, when we women began meeting in consciousness-raising groups and talking frankly about our lives, at times untangling for one another this web of confusion that forms the matrix within which abuse thrives. Like a spider, the abusive person entices the victim into his web through his ruse of love, and keeps her there, playing his game.

Based on the experiences of a great many women, feminist psychologists have documented the characteristics of this behavior pattern. A defining characteristic, for instance, is that abusers, overwhelmingly male, withhold their innermost feelings and thoughts, or are dishonest when asked to express them. In turn, they are unreceptive to their partner's ideas and needs, tending to ignore or trivialize them. They may deliberately use their partner's confidences to humiliate them in front of others. Deprived of the intimacy and companionship that is the touchstone of marriage, women in abusive relationships suffer, as I did, from loneliness.

Since abusers refuse to express themselves in an open, direct, and respectful manner, they leave their partners in the unenviable position of having to guess what it is they want, or having to decide whether to proceed on their own. Partners are then vulnerable, as I was, to having their decisions undermined or of being accused of being inconsiderate. Abusers either remain on the periphery of family life or seek to dominate it in a hostile fashion.

They strive to keep their partners isolated from the outside world. Family, friends, neighbors, and colleagues are a threat to their turf, to their control, and to their partner's undivided attention. As I made friends in our new neighborhood, my husband took to checking the sink for empty coffee cups to see if I had had company while he was at work. My wanting to visit my family once or twice a year was a symptom, I was told, of my "immaturity." Later in our marriage, if I became the center of attention at a dinner party, even momentarily, or my husband noticed me deep in conversation with another person during a social evening, he would retrieve our coats and insist that we leave. In the interest of keeping the peace, the partner may make one concession after another, but "enough" is not a word in the abuser's vocabulary.

Outsiders typically experience that aspect of the abuser's personality that was presented to his partner prior to marriage. At a time when the partner needs reassurance and support, friends' reluctance to accept that the abuser has a flip side may make the road to recovery an uphill climb, a longer process than necessary in healing the wounds.

The abuse of women is a worldwide phenomenon. Extending across class, racial, ethnic, religious, and political boundaries, it flourishes everywhere in age-old patriarchal cultures that uphold the privileges of men through sexual mores, traditional beliefs, religious practices, economic advantage, and legal codes. Each of us can help make the world a better place by supporting global efforts to eliminate the conditions that keep women trapped in abusive situations. Whether in Afghanistan or next door, being able to identify and name the kinds of violence inflicted on the bodies and spirits of women is a vital first step.

Meghan Sayres

Late for Tea

Meghan Nuttall Sayres lives with her husband and three children in Valleyford, Washington. She is a tapestry weaver who spins and dyes the wool of her sheep with natural dyes. Her first poetry collection, Between Deserts, *explores connections between the American West, western Ireland, and central Turkey (Salmon Poetry). Other books forthcoming include* Taipeis Gael: Weaving a Future from Our Past, *an oral history about a weaving cooperative in Gleanncholmcille, Donegal, Ireland (Cork University Press).*

She is author of two books for children, When Rocks Speak, *on rock art preservation around the world, and* The Shape of Betts Meadow, *a poem about a wetland restoration project in eastern Washington. Both are slated for publication in 2002 by The Millbrook Press. She holds a graduate degree in international rural development.*

AS I PEDALED UP MY DRIVEWAY, THE SOUND OF GRAVEL
crunching under my tires startled an animal in my field. It lifted its
brown-gold face above the alfalfa.

It stood in the place white-tailed deer usually come out of the woods.
But it didn't carry itself like one. This animal looked stockier. Must be a
coyote, I thought next, though its neck seemed thicker, its snout pudgier.

My bike vibrated beneath me. Afternoon sunlight wove dark shadows on the ground through a curtain of pine and fir trees. I couldn't
see the creature clearly.

The animal crouched, as if waiting to spring. My heart leaped. Was
it a cougar? I saw myself splayed between the furrows, ribs exposed, my
flesh dripping from the fangs of this cat, its huge paw pinning my face
to the soil.

The house, a thousand feet away, seemed farther than ever. There
was no question in my mind who could run that distance faster.
I prayed the glint of my spokes would intimidate it.

My skin prickled. Nerves surged that hadn't twitched since the
Pleistocene. Adrenaline rushed, muscles burned, wheels turned. I was
wishing mountain bikes came equipped with spears.

Again the predator moved and I thought I saw the absence of a tail.
My God. It's a bear! Right in the middle of my field.

I calmed down. The bear wouldn't come near. But my pulse
still surged.

When I reached the porch, I dropped my bike on the lawn, dashed
into the house and rummaged through a drawer for a monocular.
I hurried outside for a closer look. The animal swung its head. I was
wrong. This bear had the snout and upturned ears of a coyote. Its
pelage was mostly beige, with a hint of red and a splash of black. While
coyotes can be helpful by hunting moles and mice, this one made me
anxious. Death twitched from the tips of her ears.

I should have been on the road to my children's school for a Mother's Day tea. And I needed to shower. But I couldn't leave without trying to scare off the coyote. Her focus seemed to be the baby lamb in my pasture.

A neighbor later remarked, "I'd have taken care of that coyote with my Winchester." But because my notion of a neighbor includes wildlife, I could not consider this option. I figured, however, that the years I spent in college ought to be good for something. Hadn't I taken a "Strategic Planning" class? Surely something I had learned was applicable to outsmarting a coyote. Especially one who was missing most of her tail. How clever could she be?

I watched that coyote and she watched me as she stole among mice and mole. I considered the predation lore: "Their diet is largely rodents," say environmentalists. "They eat sheep and calves whole," ranchers say. But I know coyote stalks somewhere in the middle, and even a leg of lamb would be too much for me to bear. I am this bottle-fed sheep's shepherd, *its mother*.

The coyote didn't run in circles, or back and forth with its tongue hanging loose like some dogs who pester my sheep. She carried herself with feline grace. The more I watched her watch me, it became clear that this coyote had something I didn't—a perpetual hunger pang and plenty of time on her paws to appease it. She was here to stay. Even worse, I sensed she knew I did not have time on my side today. It was as if the coyote had staked out these acres before. She knew the rhythm of my life.

"Had you arrived *any other day*," I said to the coyote, "I'd outwait you. But today, I have a tea to attend."

Running to the barn, I waved to my flock of three with one hand and raised an index finger to my lips with the other. "Shhh, hurry in!" I gestured. To my surprise the lamb called "maaa" only once. The ewes ran to me without a sound. I locked them in their open-air shed. *Out of sight, out of mind*, I hoped.

I flew into the house. Taking the stairs two at a time, I grabbed my son's AM/FM CD player, ran back to the barn, and plugged it into a socket. Deejay talk echoed off Douglas firs. Rap music sang through each sprig of alfalfa. *I'll fool her*, I grinned. *She won't come within fifty feet of this racket.*

Back in the house, I stripped off my biking clothes, jumped in the shower, jumped out, and peered through the bathroom window. Ms. Death lorded over the pasture, taking the rap music in stride.

What unearthly sound could I make to scare her? My mind raced as I wrung my hair dry with a towel. Within reach was a handheld Jet Pro 5,000 blow dryer. *That's it!* I cranked opened the sash and aimed that awful sound right out the window, *Reeeeeeh. . . .* The appliance screamed its own rendition of Ernest Thompson Seton's *Coyote Song*— *I'm a vocalized tornado; I'm the shrieking of the damned.*

The coyote looked up. She must have been too far away to get the full effect. She didn't run. She didn't so much as flinch. In fact, she dropped into a semisquat, the scent-making stance for hunting and eating. "FOOD: THIS WAY," she sprayed. Then she loped a few paces closer to the barn.

"I've got an idea," I thought. Hustling into my dress, I flicked a comb through my hair, grabbed the keys, and made for my pick up. Revving the engine as loud as it could go, I steered the cherry-red nose of my Toyota onto the driveway. The clock on the dash told me I was now twenty minutes late.

I rammed the gear shift into 4WD like my neighbor might kick a shell into the barrel of his 30/30. "No mutton for *your* Mother's Day meal," I muttered as I charged out into the field, tufts of alfalfa flattening under my wheels. Weeds snagged the grill. I bounced and jostled.

The coyote looked at me in disbelief and ran toward the pines. I didn't let up. She glanced over her shoulder. Our eyes locked just before she hurdled a fallen tree and scurried up the bluff. "You won this time," she seemed to say with those oyster-colored eyes.

Turning the truck around, I rambled out of the field, reluctant to leave, though I knew I had to let go. As a shepherd and mother, I could not always be there for my young. After all, the coyote's real game begins at sunset.

Kathryn Howell Anders

Finding a Friend

Kathryn Howell Anders writes, paints, and has taught secondary English and journalism for twenty-eight years. She works with students to uncover their individual giftedness, and always completes whatever assignments she creates for them. She encourages her students to write and publish by example. Kathryn was selected by USA Today *to its All USA Teacher Team 2000 for outstanding teaching.*

She has always loved photography, an interest handed down to her by her parents and grandparents. She has written for magazines and newspapers and composed lyrics for her husband's music. Kathryn lives with her husband Elliot in southern California.

I TALKED TO MY BODY ON SATURDAY
You know, for a long time we weren't friends
Now that I look back
I'm not sure why

I think I expected her to be something she wasn't
Just like my family expected me to major in business
"Stay in business; that's where the money is"
"But, I like to draw, I like to daydream..."

So, I passed that on to my body
She was the only thing I could boss around
I could stuff her, work her, hide her, hit her
And she had no one to complain to

I looked back through a photo album
A week ago
I felt sad
Sad, because we were never friends

She was pretty and well put together
When I think back
I recognize that others
Thought she was too

But I didn't pay attention
I didn't listen. We didn't speak
I wanted to be in control of something
Someone

She always supported me
She never complained. She did what she was told
I never noticed the gift she was

Now that I'm older
I look for different things in a friend
I realize that patience and trust
Are more important than control

I see her in a new light
I appreciate her faithfulness
Her strength
Her willingness to ride my anger

I think we are becoming friends
I'm paying more attention to her
I'm letting others notice her
I'm taking better care of her

We're not best friends yet
But the potential is there

Maggie Jamison

Life Is a Parking Place

Maggie Jamison, Ph.D., is a psychotherapist in private practice on Washington's Olympic Peninsula. She is a graduate of the University of Washington and Columbia Pacific University. She finished her Ph.D. at the beginning of the second half of life, focusing on gerontology, thanatology, and depth psychology. In her life and with her clients, she weaves in Jungian psychology with her training in Integrative Body Psychotherapy.

Her passions include fiction writing, although her nonfiction articles are published more often than her short stories, plays, and poetry. She fully utilizes the natural beauty and geography of the region by hiking, cross-country skiing, sailing, kayaking, and clam digging. She is happy to report that she has been alive for sixty-four years.

RIGHT UP THERE WITH THE THRILL OF FEELING THE earth trembling as I kissed a long-searched-for lover is the realization that I am old enough now to taste and swallow the notion that time

93

has no meaning when it comes to what really matters. Living life on life's terms and expanding one's inner world are concepts in a universe of timeless dimensions. Those ideas require a very large parking place. I've looked hard to find it.

A stunning part of the search is facing one of life's requirements: admitting my past includes events that occurred thirty or forty years ago when I was still young, but inescapably an adult. Since I frequently feel no different now than I felt when I was drifting along in my late twenties and spilling into the thirties, it is a shock to look behind my back at the calendar when it flashes a toothy grin at me and nods, "Yes, uh-huh, remember the time you and that earth-shaking lover devoured sweetbreads in the intimate French restaurant in Montreal and you didn't know what part of whose anatomy passed between your lips? Well honey, for your information that was four decades ago."

I gasp, stunned and amazed. I recall hearing old people reminiscing about something they did forty years ago as adults. I wondered then if I would ever be *that* old, with memories of adulthood dating back forty years. Am I there? The ground beneath my feet suddenly feels shaky. I tape the calendar's mouth shut and reflect on how lessons learned remain sharp and vital, making the years collapse in on themselves, leaving time passed with no solid substance.

One of those lessons was learned once upon a time, in a land far away and long ago. I was climbing the dual ladder of expanding my professional skills and snagging a man, and I stumbled upon what looked like a lucky ladder. I signed up for a course in mind management. I had no idea what mind management was, but my curiosity (and my lust) had been piqued by a guy who led a week-long human relations training session I was attending. He was way too handsome, appealing, and bright to ignore. Over a lunch that I had adroitly arranged, he informed me what I was planning to order, seconds after

I delicately placed my menu down on the starched table linen. He paused, for effect, then continued his revelations, saying he had known by the first morning's coffee break that I would invite him to lunch. I squirmed uneasily at this apparent ability to read my thoughts.

After he polished off a spinach salad without bacon bits, which he declared clogged the channels in his mind as did all animal flesh, he informed me that he taught a course in mind management, and urged me to attend. He said he knew I would be really good at this work. Silently, I vowed to give up meat to clean up my mind. A heartbeat later, he smiled warmly and gently said not to be impatient about the time it would take for the effects of being a lifelong carnivore to wear off. As we spooned our zabaglione, he beamed his bedroom eyes down the front of my sweater and said, "I know what you're thinking. You're right. I am single."

I began at that moment to practice emptying my mind. I dumped all thoughts about his brown, inquiring eyes, my wet panties, and quick trysts in broom closets and declared my willingness to sign up for the course. The timing was awkward since he was talking about the intricacies of preparing crème brûlée, but I wanted to say it aloud before he snatched my thought away from me with another mind-stopping observation.

When I was back in my tiny office, out of the circle of his charm, I did wonder what I had signed up to do. I had no real information about what the course offered. I was distressed about my rapid decision, but being with him and watching him was all I wanted. On the way home that evening, I dropped by the library and picked up a vintage copy of an Escoffier cookbook. I would master crème brûlée in case he should just happen to be in the neighborhood. Cholesterol hadn't been invented yet. Opulent food and exquisite lovemaking weren't at the top of most people's list of things to be scared about in those days.

Soon, a map and registration form arrived. A new chapter to be written, a whirl of blank pages flapped around me. The course was offered in a private home about sixty miles from where my three children and I lived. After a full day of teaching, and leaving the sitter in charge, I drove those sixty miles, eating my dinner from my lap as I dodged frenzied drivers trying not to perish in rush-hour traffic as they headed home for a plastic-tray dinner, and parked in front of the TV, where the days' horrors served them their version of relaxation.

The sessions were to last four hours each evening, and we would meet four weekday nights for two weeks. I viewed it as a draconian vacation from eight nights of third-grade new math, mashed peas on the soles of my feet, Jell-O fights, and an assembly line of water glasses moving to and fro after the final kiss good night. I could do this drive, these late nights, I reassured myself. As long as the sitter didn't bail out.

I arrived without taking any wrong turns, a miracle in itself and surely a good sign. I trudged up the softly lit gravel path, winding between small stone pagodas perfectly placed on glimmering white, raked-sand patches, graced by drooping cedar boughs. The air was still. My heart pounded as I tapped the heavy Japanese bell in the entryway. Quickly I brushed the dinner droppings off my coat just before the heavy cherry door opened. There he stood, and when he saw me, he bowed deeply. I gaped! He stood aside and I tried to glide in through the doorway. He motioned to me to remove my shoes. Black tights with a hole at the top of my left big toe and nowhere to go but forward.

We entered a room bathed in soft light and filled with nine people sitting in a circle on the floor. The house's owner was a fatally gorgeous woman in a flaming red wool dress, her face framed by glistening black hair, her brilliant matching red lips smiling right down my throat. Why else could I suddenly not swallow or breathe? She introduced me to the others, ordinary people like me, all of us novitiates, trembling in the presence of this dashing duo. I knew my place.

I tried to disappear into the complex designs swirling all over the oriental rug. We spent some time introducing ourselves, and, by the tea break, I was forced to revise my goals as I watched the air space between the leader and the woman of the house quiver and crackle with sexual ferocity. I could see I was climbing one ladder, not the two I had planned; the romance ladder was entirely occupied by the expert climber in the red dress. I took small comfort when I realized I could read the scene playing out in front of my scorched eyes and I had only just begun the course in mind management. At another level, I had also learned that I wasn't the only one feeling like a mushroom sitting in the dark in a pile of fresh, steaming cow pies. My gorgeous, spoken-for friend began a brief lecture on communicating with plants as an entry point into mind management. I wondered if I could find the door I had entered as an exit point.

I sat and tried to listen, ignoring his physical allure. We tried many routes to getting our minds into the alpha-wave-length pattern that would allow us to penetrate the depths of living things. One fellow pilgrim kept dipping too deeply and landed squarely in delta state, his snoring snagging the rest of us back into beta. We floated through the evening along various meandering streams. Despite my initial skepticism, I was launched.

On the way back to my apartment, my mind was stuffed with the experiences of the evening. The black ribbon of highway stretched out in front of me like a promise of the good that would surely follow if I could just descend, or was it ascend, into an altered state and travel around in other people's bodies. The primary purpose of this skill was to help people find out what physical ailments they were burdened with and predict which bodily areas were vulnerable to future breakdown and potential disease, hence giving them control over their lifestyle choices. And, the trainers tossed out casually, being able to know what others were thinking and doing in their bodies might be useful information for other reasons, strictly personal ones. But we were admonished not to use this skill for negative or destructive agendas.

Each evening after a long period of meditation in the lotus position, which left me numb from my hips to my toes, we scurried along the pathways in our minds, looking first at inanimate objects from the inside out: forests, lakes, houses, bigger buildings, farms, and mountains. We skipped the Grand Canyon and moved right on to living creatures, peeping first into the inner workings of simple worms, then frogs, and upward on to the more developed species: pigs, sheep, cows. Someone tried a bull.

The next-to-last night, we were instructed to inventory the interiors of our workshop buddy. Had I known that I would be asked to wander about in my buddy Diane's size-22 body, I would have done some prepatory calisthenics.

During the final evening, I, my self, and my mind imagined we entered into the body of Diane's aunt and reported back that she had long, dazzling magenta fingernails, a propensity for lower-back trouble, arthritis in her knees, and if she didn't stop smoking, emphysema in her future. Diane was astonished that I could have "seen" her Aunt Mona's fingernails, and I was anointed on the spot as a fully credited graduate. I fetched my mind from Aunt Mona's body and trudged out into the night, knowing that I could detect fingernail polish on a person I had never met. On that final drive home, I decided to keep my abilities a secret from my colleagues and my family.

Feeling sheepishly ebullient about my success, I decided to try playing with my newfound skills. I noticed, with some chagrin, that my new skill had not turned me into a beautiful princess, nor had I become noticeably brighter, and I hadn't become Guinevere to my instructor's Lancelot. Still, I had completed the course, and surely something good would come of my hard work, determination, and suspension of my senses. As a fully accredited graduate, my goal became a humble one: to create parking places when I needed them.

It began to work! I was so thrilled and inspired that I decided to become scientific about my newly developed ability. I kept records of my success rate. At first it was only 40 percent of the time, less than chance. Still, it pleased me enormously when I would find a place right in front of the post office door or the drugstore. Soon, my success rate improved.

When I approached 90 percent, I began to notice a subtle shift in my thinking. I began to understand the importance of knowing what I wanted. It probably had nothing to do with the fact that for years I had been examining my inner life, traipsing hither and yon to week-end workshops on enlightenment and self-improvement, reading the latest New Age spiritual flashes in the pan. Phrases like "Don't push the river," "Chop wood, carry water," "Live in the moment," "Accept what is," and "Life gave you lemons? Make lemonade" ravaged the landscape behind my closed eyelids during meditation.

I kept waiting for my own private mantra to be bestowed on me, but instead I heard the phrases of Chief Seattle, Clara Barton, and Alfred E. Neuman, whose "What? Me worry?" I found, in truth, to be enormously helpful. By the time I became a serious student of Jungian psychology and deeply immersed in keeping a sharp eye peeled for synchronistic events, I was up to a 97 percent success rate in getting parking places right where I wanted to have them. I was inspired!

However, I stayed out of other people's bodies. I was content with imaging parking places.

I never pursued the profession of helping people through the means of reading their minds and bodies. Instead, being more draped in the clothing of conformity and tradition than I cared to admit, I chose a timeworn path, plodding and plowing my way through a Ph.D. in psychology, and, after considerable effort and giving up skiing, went to work on myself with the aid of a long-suffering therapist. Soon, my therapist had enough money from me to pay her way to Patagonia, where she could track and count guanacos. I stuck with the task of unpacking my own Pandora's box and looking at those shadowy bags of vipers and unsavory phantoms that were mine. Eventually the struggle paid off and we learned to coexist with respect and cautious concern for one another.

Today, sitting in my office with those who come to see me, I pry open my heart and mind to see and hear who they are. In return, they give me humility. They are a dedicated bunch. They teach me about who they are. They remind me not to make assumptions about what is in their hearts or minds. They tell me who they are without my having to go into a trance. I've carried what they have taught me into my other relationships.

I have found the miracle of transformation that happens when someone listens, a miracle as good, if not better, than being able to talk to plants or anticipate what a person will say next. When we are heard, we discover who we are and what we think, feel, and dare to dream. Knowing who we are makes finding the road to travel easier. Direction signs, lane markings, and the yellow dotted lines show up. So do closed tunnels and washed-out bridges, and every now and then, a stop sign appears. Knowing where to park is a good thing.

I continue to find parking places exactly where I need one when I know where I want to be.

Molly Knox

To Be a Housewife:
A Feminist Choice

Molly Knox was a practicing scientist for nine years before turning her full attention to her home and family. She is a feminist by birthright, having come from a long line of strong and capable women.

The essay published here evolved out of an undergraduate's comment, made to a faculty member at the University of Washington. The student was pregnant and intended to stay home with her child. Because of this decision, she felt it necessary to drop out of the women's studies department, as she felt being a housewife was not consistent with being feminist. The faculty member was shocked and, being friends with Molly, asked for her help. The essay was first presented as a lecture to a University of Washington women's studies class in spring 1998 and again in fall 1999. It also won first prize in the 1998 Des Plaines/Park Ridge NOW Feminist Writers' contest. It is Molly's first nonscientific paper to be published.

I AM WELL EDUCATED. I AM FEMINIST. I AM NOT religiously or socially conservative. I am a housewife. All of my peers, my educated and feminist friends, have careers outside the home. Let me reiterate that: I do not have a single friend who is completely employed at home, as I am. That can be a very isolating fact, one that requires me to reach deep into myself to find my self-worth. I certainly do not believe that all women ought to stay at home. But I do believe the work is valuable and that women and men ought to have the choice. The left is critical of my choice; much of the rest of society is critical of the mother who chooses to work outside the home and leave her children in childcare. It's up to us to change those judgments.

Before this time, I was a scientist. I produced experiments that provided data from which I drew conclusions and wrote papers. It was exciting and rich and rewarding, and also not rewarding and boring at times. There was a great separation between my work and my home, between my public and private lives. It was often hard to keep both of them organized and sane and healthy. After I had a child, I decided to stay home with her for one year. My life grew into my work, and they were integrated and sane and healthy. I realized I was happy so I decided to stay home a second year. Then my life became my work and the work was directly related to my family and other people whom I love. I loved it, except when I looked outside of it for recognition. What I do is not societally sanctioned. I am often asked when I will go back to work. I've been told I'm too intelligent to stay home, too feminist to be financially dependent on a man.

Which brings me to the name problem. Names or titles can confer respect or disdain. They also reflect our sense of identity. We all know this. It's why we go to such trouble to differentiate ourselves as Ms. Jane Jones or Mrs. John Jones. It's why some use African-American or Native American monikers rather than historical, European names that have come to represent continuing disrespect. The most important task we face in life is the formation of an identity, and a job title goes a long way toward making one feel comfortable and proud of that identity. What I do has no name, or at least no name that does not carry with it a host of derogatory or antifeminist connotations. I may be a housewife, a domestic worker, a homemaker. I have called myself a full-time parent, but that is an understatement of what I actually do.

The most important work I do now is parent my daughter. Mainly, we talk. Children have a lot to talk about and a lot of questions needing answers, and it can take all day. We've talked about outer space and what it is made of and how people can get there; she was very concerned with how they get back. We spend a lot of time outside and so she knows the names of the common birds we see and many of the insects. She's very interested in people and emotions and relationships. We know most of the words to the songs from *The Sound of Music* and spend time singing them. We visit friends and run errands. We go to the library. We both love to read. She loves all kinds of stories and I love all kinds of news and literature. She sees me living my life. She sees me gardening and cooking and building things and supervising the roofer. She sees me arguing with someone and then resolving the argument. She herself spends whole days arguing with me and I argue back. She sees me laughing and loving and angry and frustrated and dealing with it all, or at least most of it. She is by far the most consuming and rewarding work I do. And yet she is the transitory work in my life. She will grow up and move away. The rest of my work will stay and I very well may stay with it. Most people assume that when she starts school I will "go back to work," but that belies what I really do.

The most obvious work I do is to produce food. I grow all the vegetables and many of the fruits we eat year-round. I store onions, garlic, potatoes, and squash for the winter. I freeze peas, corn, peppers, zucchini, raspberries, and blueberries. I can pickles, beets, and jams. I dry tomatoes, onions, and apples. And of course, I cook. I cook really, really well. I bake all of the bread we eat. I also grow herbs and put in annual flowers just for the beauty of it.

Beauty. That is a large part of the reason I'm happy doing what I do. I get to create beauty. The food I grow is beautiful, as is the food I cook. A few years ago I built a large garden of raised beds filled with flowers and herbs and rocks. Most of the furniture in our home was made either by me or my husband. I've made sliding boards and swings and a treehouse for my daughter. I sew when I have long rainy days, mostly things for my dress-loving daughter or gifts for friends, but also curtains for the house or clothes for me. Beauty.

Autonomy. No one tells me what to do. I make my own choices and schedule and mistakes. I must tell you I am never bored. There is no boredom when you make your own work. I have enormous personal power, which brings me to a key point for all of us. What caused women to turn away from our role in the home was not the work. It was power. We needed power. And we came to believe that the way to get power was to do what men do. But that's a lie we've seen exposed by the millions of women passed up for promotion or sexually harassed. Power comes when we demand it and believe we deserve it. Certainly breaking down workplace barriers is vitally important. But so is breaking down barriers at home. I am an equal partner in the life my husband and I have chosen. We share a passion for our work and a responsibility to our choices. Without his income, our lifestyle would not be possible. And without my work and product, it also would not be possible. We chose this life together and together we make it happen.

Choice. Isn't feminism really about choice? And shouldn't all women and all men have the right to choose their work and be supported for it? One can be supported in work by a paycheck and also by a general recognition that the work is valuable. I do not get a paycheck, but this is not true all over the world. In France and Denmark, parents are paid a stipend for childcare that can be used either to pay a daycare center or to pay yourself to stay at home. It is not need based and therefore carries no social stigma. I firmly believe that such a stipend would encourage parents to consider staying at home, because receiving a paycheck drastically increases one's self-worth. If we value the role of parents in shaping the future of our society, then it does not seem like a radical thing to offer them wider choices for their individual family needs.

The paycheck would go a long way toward making me and people like me feel better about our role in society. But in the absence of that great symbol, I have learned to seek my support where I can find it. I have learned to gather strength from those people in my life who understand and support my choices. And I have learned to find confidence within myself. This can be challenging, but what is this struggle for a healthy ego anyway? Isn't it a fight we all face no matter our choices? And isn't it a worthwhile fight? I have a friend who told me after her first child was born that she felt the need to return to her job because she didn't know how to feel good about herself in any other context. Yet her self-confidence has been a constant problem over the intervening six years. Returning to her profession did not enable her to avoid the issue of her low self-esteem. By facing the challenge of self-esteem, I have grown and become more of who I really am and not simply what my culture demands of me.

Which brings me to culture. Culture will become what we make it. I believe that finding something you love and living your life with deliberate choices that reflect that love will enrich our culture. For the past 150 years, the cultural force of feminism has been a transforming power within America. Women have changed virtually every aspect of their relationship to the economic and private worlds. But we are not done. Feminism is a process, not an end point; it is not perfectly evolved. By rejecting what was traditionally women's work, we have cut ourselves off from our history. And we have created a society in which women feel ashamed to work at home. To choose to be employed outside of the home because it is satisfying and important to you is a wonderful thing. To choose it because you would feel invalidated in any other role is not.

Some families are changing our culture. I know one where the father works a four-day week and spends the other three days at home. The mother teaches one math class every morning and spends the rest of her day at home. She is extremely fulfilled, both by her teaching and by her work at home, but most important to her, by the balance between the two. I know another family of two women and their daughter. Both women work full-time outside the home and both are happy with their work. They both feel that they would not be happy doing domestic work. Because they are happy and satisfied, they provide a happy and satisfying home for their child.

My sister is a successful geochemist and her husband stays home. His work is similar to mine, except he has three children to care for. Many people have an immediate response to this situation. Some think, oh that's so cool, an alternative family, a nontraditional household. Why don't these same people think what I do is cool? Isn't this sexism? Others think, what's wrong with that guy, why isn't he working? Many people think a man working at home is simply not a real man. They may think he is lazy or controlled by his spouse or otherwise weak. Isn't this also sexism?

Shouldn't we as members of our society feel free to choose any of these or other family-work structures? The only way to change societal attitudes is by example. All women and men have a role in the future of our culture, and we will make it what it becomes, whether deliberately or accidentally.

Most people believe these kinds of choices are available only to the wealthy. There is a pervading mythology that the American family can no longer survive without two incomes. This is proven wrong every day by many single-parent households and yet the myth persists. Certainly single-parent families cannot make the choice that we have made in my family, but within the confines of the middle class, two-parent families can and do survive on one income. They not only survive, they live well.

The median income in my county is about $39,000 per individual worker. The federal poverty level for a family of four is set at $16,055. This is a cruelly low number. More realistic figures can be found by looking at what qualifies a family for public assistance. In order to receive food stamps, a family of four must earn less than $21,000. In order to qualify for the Women, Infants, and Children program, which subsidizes families with children under five years old, this family must have an income under $30,500. My husband, daughter, and I live on his income of $50,000. I know a family of four living on $33,000. And I know another family living on $38,000. We are all living well. We are not poverty stricken, nor do we feel financially underprivileged. We own homes and strictly control our spending. We make very few long-distance phone calls. We own cheap cars. We never carry a credit card debt. My husband and I each have a monthly allowance of "fun money." We also manage to save a small amount each month. If it sounds dreary, think of the payoff: we get to live our lives the way we want to. Our lives are exceedingly rich in things that aren't on the budget: time and beauty and power and choice.

Which brings me to the subject of personality and making choices that suit the individual. My sister and I are excellent examples of why no one choice is correct for everyone. Janet is a performer by nature. She runs a successful environmental consulting firm and, in her free time, writes and performs poetry that is witty and personal. She loves being out among people and collaborating with them in her science and her art. I can't think of anything, frankly, that Janet does alone. When she takes on a project at home, she involves one or all of her three children. I, on the other hand, was born quiet, even shy. I'm happy working alone. I never liked the stress inherent in having to present my work to a public or my scientific peers. I love the quietude of my work and the satisfaction of doing it solely for myself. That's not to say I don't love people and enjoy showing off my work now and then, but I need a lot of time alone.

My sister and I have each been lucky, but more than that, deliberate enough in life to find the niche that suits us. I would find her life too dispersed and overstimulating, and she would find mine too insular and understimulating. I respect her choices; in fact I enjoy a vicarious satisfaction watching her perform in her various ways. And she's one of my most ardent supporters. When I feel doubtful of my self-worth, I call Janet and she reminds me of all I accomplish and its meaning.

I don't mean to say that the life I choose is superior to others or better for children. What I mean to ask is, wouldn't our world be a better one if more people lived out their dreams and desires? Deliberate choices lead to lives that have meaning both personally and societally. I hope my chosen lifestyle impacts the people who know me in a way that improves our culture. It used to be that women provided a large volunteer workforce that made our society run more smoothly and, I think, humanized it. They volunteered in schools and arts and politics and hospitals. They gave food and time to neighbors who were sick or elderly or had a new baby. They were the glue that joined neighborhoods together. My mother raised four children as a housewife and still found time to be a Girl Scout leader through three daughters, volunteer as a Head Start nursery school teacher for eighteen years, teach a Vietnamese immigrant family how to survive in their new community, and work weekly with a neighbor boy who was developmentally delayed. Who has time to perform these roles today? France recently cut the national work week down to thirty hours. Think of the good that would do for our culture, whether we spent the time on personal fulfillment or volunteering or simply strengthening our relationships with family and friends.

What I hope is that feminism can continue to serve us as an agent of change, and that we evolve as a society to encompass choice, autonomy, and beauty. We need lives lived with consciousness to change the world.

Carole Jarvis

A Healing Truth

Carole Jarvis is a medical transcriptionist living in Indiana. She is the mother of two sons and one daughter. Her sons are now married, and daughter Kelli is the subject of this writing. Carole is also the grandmother of two. Regular visits to Florida and the ocean top her list of enjoyable outings.

The writing of this piece was prompted by attempting to help a good friend in the grieving process. It is Carole's hope that other readers could find validation in reading her words.

TAKE A WALK WITH ME. A WALK THROUGH WORDS, BUT more importantly through a part of life. Walk with me through grief— painful grief, knock-you-down, rip-you-up-and-leave-you-for-dead grief. But remember, I said "through." You won't have to stay there. You won't want to stay there and you may not look at life the same again. I know that I don't.

People are different. Different from each other in a multitude of ways, including the ways they handle a life crisis. As a society, we measure strength in many ways, but I believe that many of the calipers used to judge a grieving person do not truly measure one's strength or weakness. Often society will allow a certain time frame to grieve, or will view certain behaviors, such as returning to work or to a "normal" life, as acceptable. That is why a grieving person, in trying to conform to society's wishes, may simply learn to mask his or her true feelings to make others less uncomfortable.

Facing death is seldom easy, and to place a measurement on the intensity or validity of one's emotions, or to make comparisons between two people's reactions to death is without any constructive purpose. Each one of us who endures the death of a loved one possesses a unique gauge by which to measure the impact of that loss to our being. How the life of one person impacts another is strictly an individual thing. When you find yourself in a reality that no amount of preparation or previous life situation can prepare you for, even the closest of family or friends cannot truly realize the scope of your trauma. We bring with us into our grief work our history—our baggage—whether resolved or not. And as we are different and unique as human beings, our history and our baggage are different. This is truth. And if we recognize this as truth, then we must be willing to recognize that each of us will deal with grief in our own way, and in our own time.

With this realization of our differences, it seems obvious that generalized time frames to grieve are futile. For too many years, society has slated that two years is an acceptable period to mourn. Many of us have listened to claims that remaining busy or having more children or remarrying will "help." Perhaps this is true for some, but more often these are simplistic solutions for complex situations.

When my ten-year-old daughter Kelli was killed in a snowmobile accident, it forced me to assess all that I valued, believed, and was—including everything that I had come *from*. Like an onion, I was peeled down, layer by layer, until I found that my foundation was in fact made of sand.

Without a strong foundation to sustain me, I learned I had to build my own foundation in the midst of chaos. During the first two years of life without Kelli, I was essentially on autopilot. Looking back now, almost ten years later, I have no memory of day-to-day living. I was simply going through the motions of life. During that time I intellectualized my loss. I read everything I could find on death and dying. At times the intense reality of grief would crash through my shell and leave me wishing I were dead.

During and after this time frame, I would attend school functions and events Kelli would have been involved in, telling myself I was seeing them "for her." I could smile and be completely together, only to fall apart on returning to the safety of my home. My foundation of sand had set the stage for me to continue being a people pleaser. I could not take a stand and say no or bow out. Without knowing it, I was seeking to please anyone, everyone—everyone except myself. It took many years of emotionally falling down and getting up, of holding onto the old patterns of taking care of everyone else, before I finally accepted that to survive Kelli's loss, I would have to ease up on myself, to stop expecting things of myself that I would not have expected from someone else, and to acknowledge and ask for help.

Grief had knocked me down—and kept me down—before it forced me to rebuild. But this time I would need a much stronger pillar to build upon. I came to realize that laying this foundation will involve diligence for the rest of my life. But I know now what its cornerstone is for me—acceptance. Given the acceptance by ourselves and others that we, as grieving people, are OK—we are not crazy—our grieving souls can then begin to heal. Until acceptance comes, all too often we use much needed energy to fight battles that we need not fight.

If you are grieving and society is telling you that after "x" amount of time your life will resume some sort of "normal" aspect, and it hasn't, then the assumption, if your foundation is made of sand, is that something must be wrong with you. If you are searching for answers that don't come, with a foundation of sand, you may feel that somehow you are unable to grasp a new "normal," or that you are "getting what I deserve."

The intense pain of grief leaves you vulnerable. Don't be hard on yourself; if you were not on a rock when this hell hit you, then it makes sense that you cannot plant your feet again as readily as some. The sand keeps shifting. Instead of beating yourself up, see grief for what it is. Much the way the physically handicapped person must work harder to accomplish what most of us take for granted, those of us who grieve must work harder to reach that emotional level of stability essential to survive.

But the good news is: *it can be done.* I know because I am still here. Healing for me began only after I began to accept my own process through grief, and found a few individuals who truly accepted what the loss of my daughter did in my life. After years of literally struggling to go to work, do the laundry, and take care of the kids, I finally came to a point where I could be glad to be alive again. Not every day. But to experience any joy was something I never expected again.

In the years after Kelli died, every day of my life her loss left me empty, sad, lonely, and missing her so much that the pain was actually physical. At her birthday every year, inevitably someone would anger me with a comment like, "Is that still hard for you?" And after the anger would come depression. Holidays were horrible, and sometimes still are, and I resented the happiness of those around me when my kids and I were sometimes hanging on by our fingernails. With every family wedding, birth, graduation, and so on, I ached to have Kelli there to be a part of it. So many times, to put on a happy face to hide the sorrow inside. Watching her friends grow up, wondering what she would look like, what she would be doing at thirteen, at sixteen, at twenty. Kelli meant more than life to me. She was the best part of everything that was good, to me. Again, remember that this was "to me." This fact is not up for qualification or judgment by anyone. It is not right or wrong. It is a truth in my life. It took nearly ten years to have the strength and insight to verbalize this. It was a victory that changed my life in many ways.

Which brings us again to acceptance. Don't try to talk a grieving friend out of their pain or sorrow. It can't be done. Please don't think a "quick fix" will make them feel better. Rearranging the furniture or going back to work is like putting a Band-Aid on a broken leg. Trust me. Know that when they are able to "live" again, they will. Grieving people do not like to be miserable. Some of us are replacing foundations at this time in our lives, and that takes so much of our energy. If you don't understand the depth of their sorrow, at the very least accept that it is real to them. Your denial or inability to accept it will not take it away. It will only make their task more difficult.

If you know someone who is hurting deeply over the loss of a loved one, use this knowledge to help them. Let them talk, or not talk; cry, or not cry; be angry, or not be angry. Ask what they need. They alone possess the gauge to measure the magnitude of their loss in their life. And know that the greatest gift you can give them is acceptance.

Kelli's life enriched me immeasurably. Kelli's death took me back to my beginning. From here I can only go forward. But not in someone else's time frame or on someone else's terms. On *my* terms, sometimes making sense only to me. And it really doesn't have to make sense to you. I ask of you only this: acceptance.

Peg Lopata

When a Boy Is Born

Peg Lopata is a forty-three-year-old freelance writer and painter in New Hampshire, with two children, a small flock of hens and a rooster, four sheep, one husband, and a cat. Her work has appeared in Mothering, SageWoman, New Hampshire Magazine, Paths of Learning, *and numerous anthologies and other publications.*

ON A WALL AT MY LOCAL BAKERY IS A SIGN THAT READS, *A boy is the problem of our times, the hope of our world. Every boy born is evidence that God is not yet discouraged with men.* I had read that sign every time I'd wait for the baker to pack up my purchases, but didn't know what it really meant until I had a son. Now I think I would amend that last line: *And every boy born is evidence that God is not yet discouraged with us, especially us moms.*

When a son is born, a woman gets the chance to see something new and foreign to herself: a boy becoming a man. If you've ever wondered, like I did when I was a little girl, what it's like to be a boy, this is your chance to find out. You might have read *Men Are from Mars, Women Are from Venus* by John Gray, but raising a son is an opportunity to visit that Mars.

Having a son has changed my mind about how hard it is to grow up female. I realized boys have it tough too. I realized also the terrible traps that my son could fall into. The kind of traps that ensnared the notorious boys of our times: Kip Kinkle, Dylan Klebold, Eric Harris. Young men, boys really, who lost the battle to be tough enough. If you have a son, you know, although you'd rather not believe it, it could happen to your boy. A mother's mind goes to new places when she raises a son.

My feminist consciousness was raised in college, but my male consciousness didn't rise until later, when my son was born. It was then that I realized no true human equality could be achieved until men challenged the shackles that bound them too, and men and women decided to raise their boy children differently. I realized I had a chance (albeit a very tiny one) to bring humankind closer to real equality. It began with me, a mom raising a son.

Of course, convincing a man he is shackled is a hard sell. If you're sitting on top of the social-status totem pole, it's hard to see or feel those shackles—but my son could. I felt them too. Every time some lifeguard eyed him hard, expecting him to break the rules. Every time he was mistaken for a girl because he sat quietly waiting for me somewhere. Every time his peers called him a wimp because he didn't find pushing each other fun, insult-humor amusing, or being physically powerful the only kind of strength that mattered.

When he was a baby, seemingly neutral in gender, I believed I could help him break those chains of "correct" boy behavior and let him be himself. Then he could go further than his dad or me and have a truly risen human consciousness. He was only a baby, just seven pounds, but I felt the heavy weight of responsibility to raise him to be who he really was, and not what others might expect from a boy.

It could have been nurture or nature, one never really knows, but I didn't have to work as hard as I had imagined. Right off, he showed me he knew exactly how to be true to himself. He did some things "just like a boy," like playing with his dad's hand-me-down Matchbox cars. But he pushed aside the toy tractors and fourteen wheelers. Maybe I was wrong about boys and their supposedly natural fascination with machines.

One spring his dad tried to show him how a lawn mower works, but he preferred to pore over the pictures in his dad's anatomy textbooks from college. We bought him skates to use on our backyard pond, thinking he'd ask for a hockey stick next, but he asked for figure-skating lessons instead. And even at ten now, he doesn't have a clue as to why other kids pick friends usually of the same gender as themselves. He picks his friends by whom he likes.

Something has turned this boy into a different kind of boy. And although there are times I wish I could get him to hit the ball right on the tennis court with me, or enjoy the company of rowdy boys better, I've realized my plan to let him grow up to be who he really is seems to be happening, and as his mother I am privy to watch this happen. Even though I have worked hard on accepting him just as he is, I admit I'm relieved to watch him climb trees, catch frogs, and love baseball—*boy things*, because I sometimes worry if he'll be able to fit into the world of men, a world that still has a pretty narrow idea of what it means to be a man.

Moms and their sons can share something adult men and women rarely can, even if they stay married for many years. A mom and her son can truly love each other unconditionally. I see that with my son I

Just a selfish State-
Qu'o

can love him so easily because, although he is male, he doesn't carry the stigma of being a member of my oppressors, as my husband does. He doesn't make any assumptions about me because I am female. The connection between us has no societal static, no hierarchy based on gender, no prejudices. This is a connection I have never been able to achieve with any man.

Raising a boy can raise the compassion of every woman for all men. It has given me the chance to see what happened to my husband when he was boy. What makes him wear an emotionally blank face most of the time, or exaggerate his know-how when he's feeling insecure, or rarely show his emotions, especially joy and sadness. It has made me realize the awful price a man pays when he stifles his tears, keeps his chin up, and turns to no one when he's lonely, because those boyhood rules cannot be broken. It has made me realize the price we all pay.) *No they Blame*

I didn't want my son paying any price. I saw a baby boy in my arms on the day he was born. But I saw something else: a person just like me. Not male or female. Just human. Maybe that's why babies look sexless, so we see their humanness first, and have to peek underneath to see their gender. Maybe it's nature's way of reminding us to not have expectations according to their sex.

To me the birth of every boy is a reminder to think of Kip, Eric, and Dylan—boys who found no safe way to vent the pain and frustrations of growing up male. The birth of my son was a chance to raise a boy with some new ideas about what it means to be a boy, and a man, and gave me renewed hope that other moms and dads might see their chance too.

Katherine Cruse

Keep the Love, Not the Object

Katherine Cruse has worked in the area of historic preservation as a researcher in Connecticut, Texas, and Tennessee. She is the author of An Amiable Woman: A Biography of Rachel Jackson, *published by the Ladies Hermitage Association.*

As an adviser to a Boy Scout Explorer Post, she canoed the Rio Grande in Big Bend National Park and backpacked the Continental Divide Trail in southern Colorado. Katherine currently lives in southern Colorado, where she writes a column for the local weekly paper. She clears hiking trails as a volunteer for the U.S. Forest Service, and is learning to ski.

Katherine is fifty-nine years old and has been married to her husband Tom since 1963. Their two children are grown and they have a four-year-old granddaughter.

YOU KNOW THOSE GIFTS THAT WERE THINGS YOU didn't need, didn't like, or just didn't want, but that came from people who love you? You keep the gifts because you love the givers. Here is my advice: "Keep the love, but let go of the object."

I had an opportunity to put this advice into practice last year, when my husband and I sold our four-bedroom house in Nashville, complete with attic and basement, to move to a log cabin in a small town in southwestern Colorado. We went from 2,700 square feet of living space to 1,300, with no extra storage space.

When we told friends and colleagues of our decision, some said, "You're joking!" and a lot asked, "Are you sure?"

"Go for it!" exclaimed the people who weren't risking anything. I could have kissed the friend who said, "I never try to change someone's mind once she makes a decision. I think there's often a critical window for some choices, and if you pass one by, it just may not open again."

The house went on the market, the contractor started the addition to our Colorado cabin, and I started sorting. I told everyone that we were liberating our possessions so that they could go and live with other people. Take the books, for example. We'd always had lots of books, all kinds of books. I thought all those books were my husband's until I actually started to sort through them. Good books, wonderful stories, some we had read several times. Let them go. Let others enjoy them.

In the kitchen were the cookbooks. How did I manage to amass so many, especially when most of them contain only one or two recipes I ever use. Ratatouille here, angel pie there, that good spaghetti sauce in another. Eventually I Xeroxed the recipes I really wanted and let most of the cookbooks go, for other cooks to hungrily peruse.

Old photographs. My father had been a professional photographer, and I had hundreds of pictures he had taken, lots of them people I didn't even know. Then there were all the pictures my husband and I had taken through thirty-five years of marriage. Be ruthless, I thought.

Keep a few and pitch the rest. Just throw them away. We don't need all those memories. Hell, we hardly look at them now. People who lose everything in fires really miss only a few things. Do we really need or want a million pictures of the baby?

We had slides and photos from every trip we had ever taken. One afternoon my husband and I poured ourselves a glass of wine and sorted through those. We kept only a few that we truly wanted to remember from each period in our lives.

We had some wonderful pieces of furniture, but most would never fit in the cabin. There was no point in offering any to our son and his wife, who already had more than could fit comfortably in their three-bedroom house. I wrote to our daughter, who shared a one-bedroom apartment with three cats, and offered her dibs on the glass-fronted cabinet that held the "good" dishes and heirloom cups and glasses, or the small oak chest, or a secretary's desk.

"Also," I wrote, "I'm thinking about selling the big round oak dining table with its seven leaves. I hate the idea of storing it and worrying about it for years, and then not using it after that. If you have a dream of owning any of these pieces, I need to know."

Her reply, via e-mail, was succinct: "No real emotional convictions about the display cabinet or the oak chest. But," she asked, "the big round table—I keep thinking how much you wanted that from your mother. I thought your emotional attachment was fairly high? Please be sure about that before you sell it. As for me, I cannot ever picture myself in a home large enough to use it."

The table had once belonged to Nellie and Gus, whom my mother met when she and my father moved to California in 1942. When I was growing up we lived two blocks away, and Nellie was my surrogate grandmother, spoiling me with foods like Sugar Frosted Flakes, the first I ever ate. She had a canary that sang wonderfully, and in her garden were little succulent plants called hens and chicks and a big holly bush that bloomed at Christmas. Her dining room was enormous, with a bay window, lace curtains, and paneled drawers and cupboards along one wall.

I remember playing with Nellie's ceramic animals and small wooden blocks under the big round table in that dining room. On the wall hung an enormous cuckoo clock, dangling long chains and weights that looked like pineapples. Every week Gus wound the clock by pulling the chains to lift the pineapples back to their original position. Gus was the first person I ever saw who made crystal glasses sing by rubbing his finger around the wetted rim. I did love that table, for its size and for the memories. But I didn't love it enough to keep it forever.

That became one of the criteria for deciding which objects to keep. If we truly loved them, or if they were truly useful, we would keep them. If not, we would release them to the universe.

We kept our daughter's dolls: one that had accompanied her to the hospital when the infected tonsils were removed; the second, Clara, I made as a Christmas present one year, along with a small wardrobe. I was never a great seamstress, but Clara had a huggable body and bright chestnut hair, and she too was loved. The third, Timothea, which my daughter had made when she was about twelve, had a cracked and scarred plaster face and tangled yarn hair, and every stitch of her clothing was sewn by hand. A great deal of love was bound up with those dolls.

A lot of things, we no longer loved. Pictures that were just decoration. We let them go. Kitchen appliances I hadn't used since I'd acquired them to prepare some exotic dish; the extra microwave oven on a basement shelf; the clothes I hadn't worn in years and probably never would; the jewelry and knickknacks given by friends and relatives. Out. If I didn't have a place for it, I was ready to keep the love and get rid of the object.

"How can you let go of *this*?" some well-meaning friend would wail. "It's just stuff," I said. "I've enjoyed it. Now someone else can." We were moving in order to enjoy the mountains, to hike and ski while we still had health and strength, not to dust our stuff. These things I had been hoarding had no place in that new life.

As the weeks went by I began to realize that all these things were, in fact, just stuff. I decried the amount of stuff we take into our homes and the greater and greater amounts of time tending to it, caring for it, and moving it around. Here was my chance to liberate myself. I gave away stuff to our kids, to friends, to our church, to Goodwill Industries, and the Salvation Army. I had a big sale, and when there was still stuff left, I had another sale. The newspaper ad read, "Good stuff. Really low prices."

The cabin was finished just before we moved in. Everything we chose to keep and bring with us fit into our new smaller space. No "stuff" went into storage. We had a window of opportunity to simplify our lives, and we took it. We "kept the love and let go of the objects," and now live surrounded with only the stuff and memories that are truly important to us. I am truly grateful.

Trish Murphy

Rapids Ahead!

Trish Murphy is sixty years old and has a bachelors degree in literature and psychology, and a masters in psychology, both from the University of Washington. She was a top-ten finalist in the 2000 Pacific Northwest Writers' Association Literary Awards contest.

Trish is a native of Washington and lives in Seattle. She worked as a writer of corporate communications and educational materials at the University of Washington and the Boeing Company for over twenty years. Recently, she took early retirement so she could work full-time on an historical novel about Irish women in the eighteenth, nineteenth, and early twentieth centuries. She has taken a trip to Ireland, met her Irish relatives, and seen the ruins of the stone cottage in which her grandmother was raised. Working on her novel, she has to watch every penny, but has never been more passionate about anything in her entire life, and feels that she is doing what she was meant to do.

"CLASS-FOUR RAPIDS AHEAD. GET READY TO DIG!" OUR
river guide Betsy shouted, standing up, her eyes alert. Betsy, a small,
middle-aged woman with the body of a teenager, loved the river and
had been guiding trips for years.

As coworkers in a corporate writing group, Betsy had invited us to
join her for a spa trip down the Deschutes River in Oregon. We agreed
without hesitation, as we had all seen the photograph on her desk,
taken as she ran class-five rapids on the Skagit River in western Washington, white water almost swamping the raft. Smiling and looking
strong in the photo, Betsy is captured in a moment of time, riding the
top of a wave that glittered and foamed against gray rock.

"Dig!" she shouted again as we entered the rapids. The raft
bounded up over the waves and then down. We paddled hard and deep,
feeling the cold spray drenching our bodies, a respite from central
Oregon's summer heat.

We had been on the Deschutes for several hours, shooting class-
two and -three rapids and drifting on calm waters. Moving through
wondrous multicolored basalt canyons formed by volcanic eruptions,
we breathed in the fresh desert air. With white-hot skies overhead, we
watched ospreys glide along the river's banks, while bucks with newly
sprouted antlers scampered up amber hills.

When we entered Wreck Rapids, I felt the same exhilaration I had
seen on Betsy's face in her photograph. Crystal drops floated against a
blue sky as we paddled furiously through the class-four rapids.

"Dig, dig, dig!" Betsy hollered when the raft fell into a deep hole.
I shouted "Yahoo!" as we rode white water that thrilled me as much as
any roller-coaster ride. Suddenly, I was transported into the air as softly
and effortlessly as a feather on the wind. I felt as though I were in a
dream—I was not where I was supposed to be. Then the wave that had
caught me and lifted me so gently out of the boat slammed me down

into the rapids. The force of the impact knocked the breath out of me and I was sucked downward toward the bottom of the river. My initial surprise turned to terror. All I could see was white water, then nothing as my baseball cap slid down and covered my face. I was in the raging river and unable to breathe. In seconds, thankfully, the life jacket Betsy had tied tightly around my waist earlier that day pulled me to the surface. Pushing my cap back so I could see, I grabbed the rope along the outer edge of the raft.

Betsy screamed, "Get Trish back in the boat!" as she clutched the straps of my life jacket.

I struggled to pull myself up and into the raft, but did not have the strength. The river, raging like a train running full steam ahead, was both sucking me down and propelling me forward through the violent white water toward clusters of jagged gray rock. Why wasn't anyone helping me!

As it turned out, Jeanne, overweight and unable to swim, and Rebecca, a swimmer in fairly good shape, had been knocked onto the floor of the raft by the same wave that had transported me out. Faye, a large woman with long dark hair, was paddling furiously to get us out of the white water. Only Ellen was available to grab the top of my life jacket, as Betsy had to let go of me to handle the tiller. Fair and blond, Ellen appeared to be in good shape but at the same time seemed fragile. My body was heavy with water and the downward pull of the rapids. Ellen was smaller than I was and had arthritis in her hands. She could not hoist me back into the boat by herself.

I remained conscious as the rapids churned around me, but felt myself separating from my body. What in the world were five middle-aged, inexperienced women doing in class-four rapids? I had thought this would be an easy spa trip, as advertised. And now I didn't know if I was to live or die as I struggled to catch my breath. I had rafted the Wenatchee River in eastern Washington and the Athabasca River in Alberta, so I was not totally new to the sport. But those times the raft had been rowed by strong young men who could lift us up out of the water with one hand if we'd gone overboard.

I kicked my feet hard as I tried once more to pull myself back into the raft. With no air in my lungs, the exertion was too much. I began to think I would have to let go. I couldn't continue much longer. Why hadn't I made myself more aware of the dangers before I took this trip? Why had Betsy taken us into class-four rapids?

I could still hear the rush of the river but had no other sensation. The sky seemed to become narrower as my awareness began to slip away. I felt completely alone in the river, realizing that no one would meet death with me if I let go. But I didn't want to die—not this way. I had imagined death would be easy, that I would simply slip away into another world surrounded by light and love. As I struggled for my life in the river, it didn't seem that easy.

I was not ready to die. My life wasn't complete. The plans I had made for a trip to Ireland, the volunteer work I wanted to do, and the freedom of an early retirement would all be left behind. I had not seen my great-niece, Madison, born five days earlier. How could I die never having held her in my arms? Did my family know how much they meant to me? I had not made out a will. I hadn't written those letters to my family thanking them for being part of my life, telling each one how special they had been in my life.

With renewed desperation, I tried again to pull myself back in. Letting go of the rope, I grabbed for a strap inside the raft. Catching it, I started to pull myself up. At the same time, the river seemed equally determined to pull me downstream into the rocks. Faye finally saw the trouble I was in and, letting go of the oar, grabbed one leg of my shorts. Together, she and Ellen hoisted my lower body up as I pulled my upper body into the raft with more determination than strength. Still unable to catch my breath, I felt myself losing consciousness as I slid face down onto the floor. "I still might die," I thought, "but at least I am out of the water."

"Undo my life jacket," I gasped. "I can't breathe."

Ellen helped me turn over onto my back, unsnapped the catches on the jacket and let it hang loosely around me.

"God, her lips are as blue as her eyes," said Ellen as she tenderly held my legs between her own while she rowed. Rebecca, soaked through, her short dark hair plastered to her face, rubbed my head when she got the "stop rowing" command from Betsy and had a free hand for a moment. Jeanne, a poet who read nothing that wasn't complicated and deep, looked like a terrified child as she dug her oar deep into the water. No one seemed to know what to do for me and I was in too much shock to know what I needed. My body shook violently.

The noon sky was bright and it hurt my eyes. My sunglasses were gone! The prescription sunglasses I had carefully attached to a new safety strap had been ripped from my face and were now somewhere at the bottom of the Deschutes. I closed my eyes and let my body rest as we drifted along with the river, which flowed more gently now. Within an hour we were at our campsite.

It was late afternoon and I pulled myself carefully out of the raft and up over the slippery rocks onto the grass. We set up our tents and, after a wonderful salmon dinner, went our separate ways to settle in for the night.

I sat outside my tent and watched the full moon as it rose over the surrounding hills, casting a brilliant white light and creating a mystical, otherworldly look to the landscape. The stars were bright and clear against the desert sky, and the Big Dipper seemed to hang right in front of my eyes. The river ran fast and loud with a white noise that did not soothe me. Afraid of never waking up again, I had trouble getting to sleep. When I finally did sleep, I dreamed about death: friends' obituaries in the paper, people sitting in churches waiting to be shot. I tried to escape in this dream, but was caught in the double doors of a church, half in and half out. The terror of the dream woke me.

I heard Jeanne sobbing uncontrollably in her tent. Having lost her only brother to leukemia as a child, Jeanne had lived with the consequences of death most of her life. She was terrified to realize she might have been swept into the river and would never see her husband and children again.

The next morning, Jeanne and I decided to go back to the town of Maupin, where we had begun our trip, rather than continue. After our good-byes to the others, we hitched a ride with a forest ranger and found a motel. Exhausted, we slept all afternoon and night, and left early the next morning to pick up the other women at the takeout on the Columbia River.

Arriving at the landing, we both found our own sunny space on the grassy slopes of the park. Watching the Columbia flow gently by, I became lost in thoughts of my familiar, safe world in Seattle.

After a while, we saw the women rowing toward us, looking triumphant and tired. A part of me regretted my inability to continue with the river trip. Another part vowed to get in better shape. And yet another part was grateful to have survived. After lunch at the park, we headed back to Seattle.

Once home, I remained in shock for weeks. My body ached, six ribs were out of place, my sinuses and bronchial tubes were infected, and I could do nothing but sleep when I wasn't at work.

Anxious to see my new great-niece, I traveled to Olympia as soon as I was able. By then Madison was three weeks old. When I walked into my nephew's apartment, the sweet scent of baby powder filled the air and I could hear Madison's soft warbled cry. Her mother, Sara, was holding her. Dressed thoughtfully in the cotton shirt and hat I had sent, Madison seemed no bigger than my hand. A thatch of dark hair peaked out from under the hat and her skin turned bright pink as she cried. Sara gave her to me. Madison quieted and fell fast asleep as I held her. She was so small, so fragile, so beautiful. I held her for hours as she cuddled against me and slept, awoke to cry for her bottle, and then cuddled against me to sleep again. How precious, this life.

Bonnita Lynne

Finding a Woman-Honoring Spirituality—and Myself

Bonnita Lynne lives in her yurt on ten rural Colorado acres. Her core intellectual interests are cultural change and spirituality, having raised a transracial family and earned a masters of divinity degree from the Chicago Theological Seminary along the way. She is in the process of seeking fellowship as a Unitarian Universalist community minister. A version of this essay is also included in the anthology she is editing, Home to Ourselves: Women's Journeys to Goddess Honoring.

WHEN I MUSE ON HOW I HAVE LIVED BEST IN MY LIFE and on how I dream of living in the future, my imaging begins with a tree—an ancient apricot tree beside the patio wall on the land in Ojo Caliente, New Mexico. It seems strange that I lived there only eighteen months yet that place defines the core things I long for in life.

The apricot tree was one of many on twenty horse-fenced acres with a sprawling adobe house about twenty miles south of the Colorado border. The main house and yard were surrounded by an adobe wall breached by old and ornately carved wooden gates. On the valley side of the yard, the wall was lower, so I often leaned there, listening to the gurgle of water flowing by in the main irrigation ditch between me and the fields, which fell away in three terraces down to a cottonwood bosque along the Ojo Caliente River. I felt securely held by the mesa that rose behind me across the highway and the hills rising before me sharply to El Negro, the mountain that dominated the skyline of my mile-wide valley. Here I felt at home.

Within the wall was a flagstone patio, snugged into an enclosed area created by the house and wall. In the wall, a wooden gate opened into the house garden, which contained a chicken coop; a windmill; and pear, apple, and apricot trees. The oldest and largest tree, an ancient queen of apricot trees, stood alongside the gate just beyond the wall. Her thick and gnarled tree-branch arm reached above the gate and out over the irrigation ditch—listening to the water. Each morning in summer, I would take my tea and my journal to the small round table nestled in the patio corner up against the house and begin my day. I was happy and felt that, along with that old apricot tree, my toes went down into the center of the earth. When my children were visiting, they would pull up a chair to talk. They said, "This is Mom's place."

From the first, my apricot tree symbolized an unreasoning abundance that risked broken limbs; so heavy was she with rosy-gold fruit that her loaded arms rested on the adobe walls in autumn.

The Goddess first came to me in that deep New Mexico land place.

◊◊◊

The house had been built around a 100-year-old cabin, now a small library at the inner corner of the L-shaped building. There, in the heart of the house, was a deep quietness where I would sit in the evening and light a candle, my own small ritual of order and meaning. I'd been five years in a time when the old gods had vanished, leaving emptiness at the center of my life.

One evening, as I mused, the little adobe room filled with warm and enfolding energy. I was no longer alone—yet this love and support were unfamiliar . . . and clearly female! It was a new experience, softer and more enfolding, different from my previous experience of spiritual presence. Now I was somehow part of her and she was all of me, a complete kind of connection and rich goodness.

◊◊◊

This sense of belonging and nurturing, of identification and confirmation, was profoundly different from anything I had experienced in my previous forty-three years. I had been born into a Wisconsin German family in which a baby girl was a source of deep ambivalence: it is good to have a healthy child; it is much better to have a son. In addition, I was a private person, even as a baby, thus a double disappointment to my mother. I preferred to be left alone in my playpen, and from an early age was known for my thoughtful watching and my constantly asking, "Why?" Just not an easy and comfortable child.

In this conservative Protestant German culture, men were "normative." As a little girl I felt defective and shut out. No matter how hard I tried to be a good girl, I was never quite OK. There was something mysteriously "wrong" with me; I couldn't figure it out and had a deep sadness. This innate childhood sense of fundamental difference and inadequacy, of non-okayness, happens to be the description of shame given by John Bradshaw in *Healing the Shame that Binds You*: "To have shame as an identity is to believe that one's being is flawed, that one is defective as a human being. Once shame is transformed into an identity, it becomes toxic and dehumanizing."

I didn't have any cultural honoring of myself as a girl baby. At the root of my early Christian culture were songs honoring the birth and life of a boy baby and endless images of mother and boy child. There were no songs rejoicing in a daughter. There weren't any mother-and-girl-baby pictures. Nearly all my storybooks were about boys, and my twice-a-week trips to the movies gave me images of female possibility only through a male-generated lens.

As a young woman I derived my sense of desirability from male responses to me. I derived my identity from my father's and then my husband's name and male-defined class status. I learned to always focus my love and desire for love on a male. At school and church, I had to assume a white-male perspective in order to learn. With every breath, I had to affirm the white-male cultural perspective in order to be heard and perceived as sane.

It was as if I had been co-opted at birth. Fortunately, I did have the ability to at least partially "make it," because I was intelligent and learned to play the dominant cultural social games quite well. At the same time, these acquired habits continued to block me from knowing my own woman person and from being a healthy mother, especially with my two daughters.

Since this dominant culture required assimilation as a male-defined white woman, I found myself in a double bind, not being allowed to love my woman self unless I psychically denied it. The Bible had taught me to love others "as myself," but my culture told me to notice myself only after my daddy and my brother. Loving and being proud of myself, risking putting myself as a woman first—these were offenses to the men who defined and controlled my life.

When I listen to women around me even now, I realize that many of us were conditioned to denigrate ourselves and prevent such offense. I recently heard the following statements from three different women in a one-week period: "I never trust a woman," "I hate working with women," and "Oh, I would never listen to a woman [minister]!"

Such painful and confusing words to hear. I am a woman; I am ordained clergy (in a non-Christian denomination). Am I really so abhorrent? What alienation many of us still carry—and impose on other women.

Along with male-translated self-identity, trust and love, I also absorbed spirituality secondhand. In church, only men talked and actively participated. My Protestant spiritual images were all male except for the Holy Spirit/Ghost. Yet the Spirit was certainly never pictured as a woman next to the Father and the Son. My favorite book of the Bible as a little girl was the Book of Esther, the story of the commoner turned queen, who risked her life to save her people. And I privately envied Roman Catholics their Virgin Mary, Our Lady of Guadalupe, Saint Bernadette, and Joan of Arc.

◊ ◊ ◊

Theodore Runyan in *What the Spirit is Saying to the Churches* writes, "To trust God is to be enabled to trust oneself at the very core of one's being. . . . Once we have been grasped by God's affirmation of us, we have experienced love at the very heart of things. And the power of that love begins to make all things in this fragmented world whole again." As a religious woman, I kept trying to be OK and trust a male god, even achieving a seminary degree in my late thirties. For all those years, I did experience God as a strong, loving, and supportive male presence—but that was never enough to make my fragmented life whole. No matter how smart and hardworking and enthusiastic and caring I was, I could never quite get there. I still felt "other" than male God, still less than male history and leadership, still in fundamental shame.

During those seminary years, new doors opened in my mind when I read Mary Daly's *Beyond God the Father* (such a psychic and physical shock that I was sick for two weeks) and *GynEcology*. And an early empowering moment came when a male seminary professor asked about my theology, responding to my feminist statement with, "Oh, special-interest theology." I somehow took unfamiliar courage and responded, "All theology is special interest. You need to acknowledge the presence of *your own* special interest." I had finally begun to stand on my own female ground.

However, with my male images gone, I found myself in a spiritual void. Where was I to experience a female-centered "image-in-nation"? I finished seminary simply as an act of will, left my intentional Christian community when I found myself becoming bitter with frustrations as a female leader, and took myself and my younger children to the mountainside in northern New Mexico to heal. Here is where I found my apricot tree, and the Goddess found me.

At first I didn't have any cultural understanding of the woman strength, honor, enfolding warmth, and sense of nurture I was experiencing. Yet that moment of glorious and good female presence in a little adobe room finally gave me permission and possibilities to be whole as a woman. Over time, I have met multiple Woman-Goddesses, found some profoundly loving stories and pictures, felt defended by Woman Warriors of strength and inspiration, and been enriched by Hispanic,

African, Native American, Nordic, Polish, Celtic, Chinese, and Japanese goddesses. Both one and many, She affirms me as I am, in all my woman complexity.

After living with a derivative self-image and a derivative spirituality, how clear and true it now feels to have woman spirituality and woman imagery and woman definition in the world. Centered in a woman-honoring spirituality, I am whole, I am loved, and I am challenged and nurtured from a place of basic trust, enabled to be my woman self with pride and confidence instead of shame.

Standing on affirmed woman ground, I can trust myself and another woman, I can listen to myself and other women, I can love myself and other women. Living a woman-honoring spirituality, I can love others and the apricot-tree-abundant earth, with integrity—as I love myself.

Victoria Wright

Anniversary Waltz

Victoria Wright lives in the Berkshires with her two children, Winslow, age fourteen, and Signe, age eleven. To this point unable to settle on a career, she has at various times been a private investigator, a credit manager, a general contractor, a publisher of personal memoirs, and a stockbroker— perhaps the inevitable result of a degree in philosophy. She was also the original homeschooling columnist for The Mining Company, *now* About.com *on the Internet. She is completing her first novel.*

TODAY WAS THE TWENTY-EIGHTH ANNIVERSARY OF the loss of my virginity. The event itself was not one to be celebrated (or even, if given the choice, recalled) but the milestone is worthy of recognition, I feel. The real highlight of that night in 1973 was a surreptitious call to my best friend—honoring a promise we had sealed four years before when she, an early bloomer, had lost hers to some forgotten heartthrob on a beach somewhere. Our quick conversation was followed two days later by the "Congratulations!" she'd immediately watercolored and sent off. I still have that card.

I have always acknowledged, sometimes with a partner and sometimes alone, that day and its importance to me. Many times it has set the tone for an evening of hilarity with women friends as we lay out, with huge laughter, disbelief, and understanding, our stories in gory detail. Each of us remembers in excruciating clarity the act itself, although I have found to my surprise that I am the only one who recalls the actual date. For no woman of my acquaintance did the earth move, and for many, myself included, it was a time of dire emotional stress, as our lovers realized belatedly the enormity of what had occurred and cantered away. For some of us it was the beginning of a lifelong trend.

At one point years ago I counted the men I had been with, and came up with a number in the low two figures. A modest group, considering the times. I'm sure that either of my sisters and many of my friends could beat it. One of my sisters tells a story of a conversation she had with our mother on the subject of how many men was too many men. This talk, I need hardly add, was instigated by Mom, who must have felt that there should still be some standards. I imagine her as a British woman of the Raj, bravely trying to maintain staid Western ways in the sultry sunsets of spicy, isolated India, where people could not have been less impressed with her high-tea traditions. Mom advised that if we "had an affair" with too many men, eventually *we would regret it.* "I don't know about you," my sister said, as she told me this story not long ago, "but I'm still waiting to regret it."

So, she'd asked Mom, how many men was too many? Well, you should be able to count them on the fingers of one hand. "No problem, I told her," my sister had said to her best friend later as they'd shared a joint in the basement, exhaling through the dryer vent and laughing until they were about to pee their pants. "I can do that. But I have to use each finger six times."

After a good deal of thought, I am able to put names to most of the notches on my mental bedpost. Some of them were utterly incidental—the merest blips on my radar, passing fancies, or big mistakes. A couple were ships in the night who will always make me smile, with a twinge of real longing, when I think of them. But there are also a few faces who were passions for a time, and one or two others who may turn out to have been the heroes of my life. They are part of my past, Mom, all of them, and no, I cannot imagine feeling anything like the regret you sug-gested—for the mistakes, the missteps, or even when I fell hard.

The places these men hold in my heart don't reflect the length of time we knew one another, or even our importance in each other's lives at the time. What moves me to remember them may have little to do with who they were—their beauty or talent or character. When they wander through my dreams or break the surface of my thoughts, what comes back might be a stray remark, a laugh, or a look of love. One, now dead, always brought me a Coke when he visited. Another's calligraphy of the lyrics of my favorite song is still in my files some-where, and when I chance to run across it, his voice, with the lilt of the privileged South, floats through my head. A third, now moderately famous, sketched me all one summer. His beautiful body and blond, blond hair carried the faint scent of oil paint and turpentine, and my heart will always pound at that evocative aroma.

And from a last lost love I have a small packet of letters, around which I'll tie a satin ribbon someday. Those letters are breathtaking still. Twenty years have done nothing to diminish their power and when I read them I am transfixed. This young man and our sad and magical history I do regret, and it is with him I will sleep in my mind tonight, when I've turned out the lights and reviewed the parade of the past.

Dottie Moore

Quilted Stories

Dottie Moore has been a studio artist for more than twenty-five years, first as a weaver, and now as a quilt artist. Her works appear in many publications and hang in private and corporate collections in the United States and abroad.

She is passionate about the process of creative expression and its ability to transform lives. She is the founder of "Piecing a Quilt of Life," a national program dedicated to empowering senior women by recognizing their creative abilities. Her lectures and workshops are offered to groups across the country, visual artists, musicians, writers, cancer patients, and quilt artists. Her Web site address is www.creativetraces.com.

BEING SIXTY IS GRAND. I HAVE LIVED LONG ENOUGH to understand the joy of wisdom. I know that today, this moment, is what is important and that many times joy simply waits for a shift in my perception. This simple truth seems like an easy thing to learn, but

I don't think I could have accomplished it much earlier. I simply didn't have enough life experiences to trust the process.

Age and experience provide endless possibilities for discovery, and more than twenty years of quilt making has taught me to see my life as art. As I piece, layer, and stitch fabric together, I work in silence, listen to my quiet intuitive voice, and allow this voice to guide my process.

It is this intuitive voice that teaches me to appreciate and express my uniqueness. It guides me when I become stuck in a design problem, reminds me to move physically when my creativity needs to flow, and nudges me to let go of control when my breath becomes shallow or my body is tense. Following my intuitive voice teaches me to trust in the process of creation, and trust develops my patience.

Authentic art evolves one step at a time and comes from the open heart where we dare to speak our truth. When I choose to see my life as art and surrender to the process, I find that my work flows; it fills me with energy, rather than draining me. When I first began my journey as a studio artist I planned each piece before I began stitching. Then I spent countless hours trying to make the quilt fit the image. Experience has since taught me to work intuitively and to listen. I have discovered that each piece has a message of its own and that the final image may be radically different from the spark that created it.

Making quilts has also taught me the power of symbols. The trees, mountains, clouds, roads, and plowed fields in my work became personal symbols when I realized that they were representing deeper truths for my life and art. For example, trees show me how to move with the forces in my life, and their roots remind me to do my inner work so that I can reach my greatest potential. Mountains represent strength and silence. They hold the mystery of the universe in the folds and layers of their mounds. Clouds are the "ah-ha's" of life. They are the conscious thoughts floating in the vast unconscious sky. These symbols and others are in my art to teach me to pay attention to what attracts me in the world, and to ponder the deeper meaning of everyday experiences. I now know that every image that attracts my attention is there to teach me what I need to know in the present moment.

The process of creating is also teaching me to slow down, observe, listen, and sometimes do nothing. It is out of this silence that I can review my choices and receive opportunities that I might otherwise not see. For years I was so focused on the process of quilt making that I could not see what it was teaching me. Now I know that "process" is "process." By dropping my narrow definition of creative process, I am expanding my possibilities. I am now offering lectures and workshops to a broad spectrum of audiences including other visual artists, writers, musicians, storytellers, college students, and the general public.

In many ways, it feels like everything in my life has been leading to this moment. In May 1996, just as I gather fabric for my quilts, I began collecting the stories of women quilt artists over the age of fifty. I was curious to know whether other women had experienced major life changes through the practice of creating. If so, how had their lives evolved, and how had these changes affected the way they lived in community.

I was then fifty-five and, after twenty years of studio work, I no longer felt that I was creating my quilts, because I knew that the process of creating was making me. All the years in my studio were simply practice for learning how to see possibilities and make choices.

Collecting women's stories has confirmed my belief in the profoundness of everyone's life. We have all gathered wisdom that needs to be shared. Sometimes we discount our experiences by choosing to see them as ordinary, but a deeper search takes us to a place of truth where we can see and own our power. Two experiences in my life gave me this insight.

In January 1991, I packed my suitcase and loaded my car with all kinds of creative supplies. I was headed for a South Carolina beach, where I was going to spend five days and four nights with three friends. We were all artists interested in women's spirituality and we wanted to spend time together experimenting with some of the practices of rituals and bodywork we were inviting into our lives. We named our group "The Experiment." Upon arriving, Caty volunteered to prepare homemade soup for our first meal. In my usual inquisitive way, I turned to Emily and asked her something about her life as a child. One question led to another until we placed dinner on hold while all of us gathered around to hear her story.

Several hours later, after listening to Emily and having dinner, I asked Anne to share her story. These storytelling sessions expanded to include Caty and myself, and continued for five days. Waves of emotion were released as layer upon layer was revealed. Although we had known each other for several years, this was the first time we had spent long quality time together. We received the gift of listening, as we gained awareness of the power in each of our lives. We all left for home feeling light, as if a burden had lifted, and empowered by the importance of the experiences that had molded our lives.

The second experience that taught me to question and reflect on my life was in 1993. *Traditional Home Magazine* sent an editor to my studio to interview me for an article. He was intense in his questioning and kept his laptop humming for two days as he dug deeper and deeper into my creative processes. As with "The Experiment" retreat, I again experienced the cleansing effect of storytelling. With these two experiences, it is not surprising I chose to interview other women artists.

The project, which I call "Piecing a Quilt of Life," is now an integral part of my work and has grown into an international network of creative women. My intent is to honor senior women by recognizing their creative abilities and to encourage them to serve as mentors for our culture as we search for deeper meaning in our lives and ways to age creatively. Their stories are being documented through audiotape, slides, and black and white photography. Their lives, works, and wisdom are being showcased through exhibits, newsletters, and a Web site. The project also offers workshops, lectures, and conferences to encourage and expand creative expression in all of our lives.

"Piecing a Quilt of Life" connects, inspires, and empowers senior women to see the beauty of their lives. It also encourages them to tell their stories, to create their legacies, to connect with the wise women who lived before them, and to mentor the next generation.

What I love about this project is the symbolism of the senior woman and her quilts. The woman represents the wise, intuitive, creative part of each of us, regardless of age or gender. The quilts represent the individual lives we piece, layer, and stitch together. The women and their quilts mirror the many layers of meaning we create in our lives.

Quilts consist of three layers stitched together. Each layer has a unique purpose and demands careful attention to ensure the beauty and quality of the finished product.

The first layer, the foundation, is seen only when the quilt is examined from behind. Sometimes it is only one piece of durable fabric, but many times it is several fabrics pieced together to make a whole. This may have been a design choice of the quilter, or she may have had to make do with what she had on hand. The same is true in life. Sometimes our lives emerge strong, as products of nurturing parents and environments, and sometimes we have to invent ways to nurture ourselves. Both have the potential for creating firm foundations.

The middle layer of the quilt is usually hidden, yet it provides warmth, depth, and dimension. The creative woman does the same with her life. She examines and reflects on her life. She nurtures her soul. She listens and follows the quiet voices of her inner wisdom. She learns to honor the birth, death, and rebirth cycles in her life and welcomes change as an essential part of her growth. She knows that committing to these practices creates character and adds integrity to her life.

The top layer is most visible. It reflects the decisions of its creator and reveals what is important in her life. Color and design combinations produce a range of expression as varied as the women who create them.

As I gather, sort, and stitch these pieces—these stories I have been gathering—and border them with my personal experiences, I see the importance of every choice. I see how darkness allows the light to shine, and beauty emerges from the depths of the ugly.

When the women talk about their lives, I know that they are reflecting my own. When they reveal their insights, I find wisdom. When they show me their work, my soul responds. I know that I am in the presence of courageous individuals, because timid souls do not risk the vulnerability that I witness. These women have taught me to listen, to trust the process of life and art more completely, and to always see the possibilities.

The wisdom that I would share with a younger Dottie Moore is that process always produces growth and forward movement. Standing still is not an option. We can fully engage in the process of choices and possibilities in our lives or we can wait to be moved by outside forces, but even that decision is a choice. When we engage mindfully in the process of life and art, we choose to see every moment as a place of learning and awareness, and every decision as a step in creation. The joy is in dancing with the process.

Beverly Hughley

The Girlfriend Club

As a resident of south Florida, Beverly Hughley is one of those rare individuals talked about but seldom seen: the native Floridian. An avid reader since preschool, Beverly's passion for reading evolved into a thirty-year affair of writing poetry, short stories, and nonfiction essays. In 1988, after years of journal writing, Beverly decided to test the proverbial waters by entering the McDonald's Literary Competition in Essence magazine. Lo and behold, she was selected as a finalist. Believing that this was a fluke of some sort, she entered the same competition the following year and once more was selected as a finalist. As a writer with no formal training, and overwhelmed by this turn of events, Beverly went on a self-imposed hiatus from writing that lasted for nine years. Finally, in 1998, after mustering the courage to apply, she was selected as a participant at the Hurston/Wright Writers' Week Workshop in Moraga, California. From that point on, she has been writing nonstop.

Beverly is currently working on a book of short stories regarding the African-American experience from the feminine perspective, a collection of personal essays, and a book about her relationship with her youngest sister. She is a graduate of Florida International University with a degree in public administration, and lives in Hollywood, Florida, with her twenty-five-year-old son, Quentin.

IN MY OPINION, SINCE THE BEGINNING OF TIME women have borne the brunt of society's expectations of us. As the fairer sex we find ourselves conforming, trying to live up to someone else's ideal. That's where a girlfriend can step in to save us. I am willing to bet that if Eve had had a good girlfriend during her reign in the Garden of Eden, undoubtedly the girlfriend would have influenced Eve's decision to partake of the apple, thus altering the history of the world.

Good girlfriends have the knack of rescuing us at the right time, preventing our missteps, and saving our hides. As a forty-plus woman who's been duly blessed with a supportive circle of girlfriends, I can personally verify the aforementioned statement. To have a good friend, you must first be one. So, keeping that adage in mind, I came up with a list of strategies to be a good girlfriend:

• *Be a good listener.* I try to provide my undivided attention if my girlfriend needs to vent or needs a sounding board.
• *Be supportive.* If a girlfriend expresses interest in a specific area—let's say education, health, or business—I take it upon myself to provide news clippings, magazine articles, and dates and times of TV broadcasts related to the subject.
• *Provide encouragement.* Attempting anything new or different can be scary, so I encourage my girlfriends to take risks if they feel "a calling," but to always research and prepare first.

- *Plan a girls' day out.* When girlfriends are experiencing major drama in their lives, I recommend a Saturday matinee—no kids, husbands, or housework. And the price is always right.
- *Counter negative images.* Because women seldom receive enough positive reinforcement to grow and thrive, I accentuate the positive. Yes, you may have gained twenty pounds but what about that master's degree you completed this year?
- *Check in to the spirit.* When a girlfriend gets overwhelmed or feels like her life is out of control, it's time to go to church for some spiritual uplifting. Afterward, brunch is just what the doctor ordered!
- *Fantasize.* Winning the local lottery, meeting Mr. Right, or fulfilling that lifelong dream—yes, we know the odds may be against us, but a little fantasy never hurt anybody.
- *Laugh.* This cannot be emphasized enough. We must help our sisters find time to laugh at the absurdities of life, ours and others.
- *Separate the decision from the decision maker.* I may not like my girlfriend's decision, but it is *her* decision, and I will still love her.

One would think every woman would be a friend and have a friend. But this is not necessarily so. There are categories of women ineligible for membership in the girlfriend club. The emotional baggage they lug with them restricts them, and they drain energy out of a friendship. Who are these women? They are

- *Negative sisters.* Constantly harping about any and every thing. Outings are usually a disaster. Food too hot, too cold, prices too high, seating too bad, and so on.
- *Sisters with no ambitions or goals.* These women are afraid to take chances. Instead of making things happen, they wait for things to happen to them and for them.

- *Fearful women.* Sisters who view other women as threats or competition and act accordingly.
- *Rigid women.* Sisters who are uptight, unwilling, or unable to kick off their shoes and let their hair down. Every sister should do this at least once in a while.
- *Insecure women.* Sisters who throw their accomplishments (professional, personal) and material possessions (luxury car, designer clothes, jewelry) in the faces of other sisters.
- *Dangerous women.* Sisters who engage in potentially risky, life-threatening activities like illegal drug use, drinking to excess, one-night stands, and unprotected sex.
- *Dishonest women.* Sisters who'd lie just as soon as they'd tell the truth. These sisters cannot be trusted.
- *Disinterested women.* These sisters don't feel the need to connect or establish ties with other sisters. They fail to see the importance of friendships in their lives.

I was personally introduced to this last category of woman last year at a Youth Empowerment conference in Fort Lauderdale. The youth minister asked the audience of mostly African-American teens to name some important qualities that people should have.

"Loyal!"
"Trustworthy!"
"Honest!"
"Dependable!"
"Supportive!"

These were some of the responses shouted out. At that point, the minister asked for a volunteer. Several hands immediately shot up, waving with urgency.

Out of the sea of brown, tangled arms, he selected a young lady who appeared to be between the ages of fourteen and sixteen. Short in stature, with an infectious laugh and chic hairdo, she bounded out of her seat, sashayed to the front, and stood in front of the blackboard.

"What I want you to do next, young lady," said the minister, "is write down all of the important qualities of your best friend—in other words, those characteristics that make her special."

Her response surprised and saddened me. "I don't have any girl-friends," she said flippantly. "All of my friends are boys." She said that loudly, perhaps for emphasis, or to impress those of us listening to her seize her fifteen minutes of fame.

What I wondered, could make someone of such a tender age, reject those most like her?

Years before, I had heard that very same statement from a coworker. She was loud, arrogant, and pushy. It was a no-brainer to understand why she didn't have any girlfriends. My theory then, as it is now, was that she probably had alienated, betrayed, or pushed most of them out of her life. At any rate, she unknowingly and unwittingly did womankind a tremendous favor.

As I looked at "Miss Thing," clad in her skin-tight designer jeans, gold hoop earrings, and attitude for days, I still could not fathom the extremity of her views. Could they have originated from some adolescent misunderstanding among her peers? Perhaps that green-eyed monster we know as jealousy? Or maybe the classic "he say, she say" created these hard feelings she so willingly shared with the rest of us this day?

I thought about girlfriends and women friends who have been a part of me since I was me. I thought about those who encouraged me in any and every endeavor I attempted. Those who were my sounding boards during times of crisis. Marathon phone sessions that started in darkness and ended in daylight of the following day.

Thought about ten- and twenty-dollar bills pressed into my hands (amid protests), by girlfriends who were struggling financially as well. Thought about girlfriends who called long distance, or sent cards "just because."

Thought about girlfriends who believed in me when I didn't believe in myself. Thought about girlfriends who came to hen parties to grub and catch up on gossip. Girlfriends who listened and offered advice on ill-fated romances. Girlfriends who fed my body and soul.

Girlfriends who spent hours with me in local bookstores, just chillin'. Girlfriends who hung out with me in malls, browsing and eating cookies from The Original Cookie Company 'cause we were both broke. Girlfriends who walked with me in parks in another futile attempt to lose some of that middle-age spread. Girlfriends who thought my outlandish ideas had merit.

Girlfriends who listened in silence as I sobbed hysterically upon learning that my baby sister had been infected with AIDS by her wayward husband. Those same girlfriends who flanked me for seven hours in a funeral home at her wake, one year later.

Girlfriends who continue to implore me to "Go back to school, and finish that degree, because you are *not too old*!!"

Girlfriends who support my decisions to quit unsatisfying, unfulfilling jobs. Girlfriends who laugh at my dirty jokes. Girlfriends who embrace me and tell me that they love me. Girlfriends who eat and like my cooking. Girlfriends who take my side automatically whether I'm right or wrong.

Girlfriend, who, a year and a half ago, helped me select the dress to bury my mother in. Girlfriends who quickly and quietly moved in to close gaping holes left by deaths of loved ones.

Girlfriends who are black, white, old, young, bisexual, professional, uneducated, single, married—near and far.

Girlfriends support, nurture, sustain, and protect me. I shudder to think how much more difficult my life would be without my navigational system of girlfriends. I pray this is something I will never have to find out.

While male friends have been known to be supportive and caring, their very maleness, as sexist and elitist as this may sound, excludes them from entry to this most prestigious club. After all, anybody can apply, but not everyone will be accepted for membership. Besides, when I think about it, it's kind of hard to imagine a one-on-one conversation with a member of the opposite sex about newly discovered stretch marks, drooping breasts, weight gain, and that oh-so-dreaded cellulite!

To that unknown, unnamed, young lady in the breakout session, there is still hope, because time, in fact, is on her side. It is my hope that as she matures and grows, she will come to view her sisters as the valuable commodities that they are, instead of the enemy to be feared, hated, and avoided at all costs. It has been my experience that the circle of sisterhood is invaluable and enriching in many different ways, but only if one is receptive to its many gifts.

Kay Murphy

The Time Machine

Kay Murphy was born half a century ago with a formal Irish name, and has lived in the Chicago area all her life. An English major, she is a published writer, poet, and editor. Her credits include the e-book, The Schipperke Handbook *(Hoflin, 1998), nominated by the Dog Writer's Association of America for excellence in the category of nonprint media (books). Her poems have been published in* The Prairie Light Review, *and some of her essays have appeared in e-zines and literary journals.*

Editing credits include academic and scientific papers, journal articles, and chapters in a recent JAI book, Oncology of Prostate Cancer. *She is on the editorial advisory board for oncology for Stedman's, the medical reference division of Lippincott, Williams, & Wilkins, and has worked on three books recently:* Stedman's Oncology Words, Stedman's Radiology Words *(for which she wrote the lexicon for radiation oncology), and* Stedman's Medical Equipment Words. *She recently was on the editorial advisory board for their electronic medical spell checker.*

Kay is a certified clinical research professional and is on the board of directors of the Society of Clinical Research Associates and on the editorial board of the professional journal for clinical research associates, The SoCRA Source. *She is the manager of the research office at a major Chicago area hospital.*

She is a daughter, sister, aunt, wife, mother, and friend to many significant people who have come into her life over the last half-century.

DRIVING DOWN THE ROAD ON A BEAUTIFUL SPRING day, I saw her, parked perpendicular to the gravel shoulder of the road, a "For Sale" sign taking up much of her front window. I turned to my husband and reminisced, "Do you remember when I wanted a car like that so very much?"

The next morning, as I was wringing spilled coffee from a dish towel into the sink, I glanced though the window and was stunned to see her in the driveway: a fifteen-year-old, shiny, orange Fiat Spyder with a black ragtop, purchased as a surprise, no-occasion gift from my husband and extremely excited fifteen-year-old son.

My heart began to pound. She was mine! I couldn't believe it! I hurried out to the driveway in my sweats and fuzzy slippers, and ran my hands along her glossy finish. She was a three-dimensional picture from the album of my younger mind, parked there in my middle-age reality. I walked slowly along the car, back to front, touching her all the time. Then I stepped back and took a deep breath, taking it all in. It really was the car of my dreams, sitting right there in my driveway. My middle-aged self told me it was ridiculous and totally impractical to have a car like this now; my younger self told me nothing but that she was wonderful!

I stepped around to the driver's side, opened the door, and slid in. The seats smelled of leather, even though they were slightly worn and patched with electrical tape. I didn't care.

"Don't touch the car!" I found myself needlessly spouting off at anyone who came near what was really just an old used car.

I put down the top and placed the boot over it. I rolled down the windows and put up the visors. I was ready.

I started her up and she purred like a contented kitten. I reached for the gearshift, which became a mechanical extension of my arm. Although I hadn't driven stick for years, it was instinct—I was going to *drive*—not chauffeur, not shuttle. My destination was nowhere—not a practice, a lesson, or the store. I was at one with the road.

I slid her into reverse and gently let off the clutch. I backed slowly down the driveway and out into the street. She roared into first gear and I remembered that a car like this should *never* be treated gently. I stepped on the gas hard, revving the engine. Second gear, third gear, all in less than a block. I watched the RPMs rise and fall, in sync with my adrenaline level. I was driving again!

Although the heat was stuck in the on position, I could feel the cool wind of freedom in my hair. I popped Credence Clearwater Revival into the tape player and I was on the move—a move back twenty years in time. I had no children, no husband, no worries, no cares, no responsibilities. It took eight bucks to fill the tank and I could drive for a week.

But, fifteen minutes into the ride, it seemed that something was missing. So I drove back home, picked up all the kids, squeezed them into the nonexistent back seat, and took off again.

"I see the bad moon a-risin'. . ." chorused from the back seat. Surprised, I looked at the giggling children through the rearview mirror and wondered how they could possibly know the words to that song.

Lisa Barstow

Living in the Mystery

Lisa Barstow recently moved with her husband to Kennebunkport, Maine, from Amherst, Massachusetts. After spending fifty-four summers in Maine, she is proud to finally be a "year-rounder."

Her writing life began informally thirty years ago, when she would scribble random thoughts down on notepaper and stuff them into her "important drawer." After progressing to journal writing, and filling several blank books each year, she joined a writing group in 1995 and began to take this creative pursuit more seriously. In April 2000 Lisa graduated from Vermont College with a BA in creative writing with a focus in poetry, writing about the natural world, and memoir writing.

Lisa has led writing groups for teenagers, and facilitated women's groups as well. She has recently begun to lead groups for Hospice and the Cancer Community Center this year in southern Maine. She is also trained as a holistic therapist, having had an eight-year practice in Amherst.

Lisa is the mother of three grown children and the grandmother of four young children.

WHEN I ENTERED MY FORTIES I BECAME BEGUILED by inner process, the search for an expanded self, and a 'raised' consciousness. I had been propelled into change and a new life by the death of my husband three years earlier. At thirty-seven I was no stranger to death. My grandparents and parents had died years before, but this death rocked my foundation in a way that I had never experienced.

Peter and I had been married in college, and had two teenage daughters and a sweet nine-month-old son when we found out that Peter had cancer. His death, at thirty-nine, nine months later, toppled the world that I knew and brought me into a more profound understanding of life and death. It challenged the way I viewed the outer world, and most importantly, it called me into a more intimate relationship with myself. I began to realize that I had an inner life that was demanding to be seen.

I became conscious of the Mystery, or the spiritual unknown, and entered its realms. I had felt comforted by my patriarchal Christian vision of God during my childhood and young adulthood, but now my belief had expanded and deepened to include what I couldn't understand with my rational mind. I worked hard to improve myself, to find more meaning in my life, and as a result I was drawn into a holistic way of living. I enrolled in a training in body/mind therapy so that I could bring my new awareness to others.

During personal therapy sessions and silent meditation I dove into the Mystery pretty deeply at times, uncovering from my unconscious mind images and thoughts that held information from my past. I thought that if I could just uncover one more piece of family history and the impact its system had had on me, then at long last I would be "done" with this quest of mine and I'd be able to get on with my life.

I have learned, however, that when one enters the Mystery, there may be a beginning but there is no finish line, no end to reach. Experience and maturity have taught me that the images given us by the Mystery are not linear but rather a continuum, like a spiral. Now, at fifty-six, I walk the spiral, descending deeply into the process of becoming a more integral part of the whole. The quest has shifted from just a personal cause and expanded beyond into the collective. I believe that the spiral is one of the Mystery's mandalas. It allows a circular route for the mind of the traveler to descend or ascend. When I close my eyes and "go inside myself" I am on the spiral and feel as though I am being submerged into an archetypal realm.

At times I would feel afraid of the unknown and what might be thought of as the dark side of the Mystery. But I would seek comfort in knowing that I was traveling the spiral. I was working hard on myself, after all. But when I would sense the inherent danger of descending too deeply into the psyche, I would quickly come up for air, giving my process some space from such focused attention on the self. Now, I have grown the faith to stay under for a while and to trust that I will learn to breathe in the places of the Mystery, where before I was afraid I would drown.

The Mystery guides me. It is where my intuition lives, it is where the alchemy of fear transforming into love exists, it is where I can connect with an energetic force that is in all things. I believe that it is what we call God. I trust where the Mystery takes me, and while I know that I have free will, I try to be present and listen so that I may hear its call. In my thirties and forties I didn't want to allow the flow of the Mystery to steer me down the river. Indeed, I would have images of being in the water and holding onto a branch on the bank for dear life, afraid to let go and see where the river might take me. It is easier to trust now, even when I cannot see what is around the next bend. The boundaries and conventions that often gave the illusion of safety and control are not as clearly defined.

This is not to suggest that I no longer feel fear or confusion, or that I have given up my need to control. My life can be volatile at times and yet now I try to remember to ask the Mystery for balance when I am not feeling attuned. I am learning that there won't necessarily be an answer for every question that I ask because often it is enough just to ask the question. Then there are times when I feel stripped clean of expectations and my inner house is bare. I am left with all the knowing that I have collected, and like being in the river, it is time to let it go. Sometimes I feel frightened because I cannot see what lies ahead, and yet I am comforted by an acceptance of the moment that comes when I am able to surrender control. I have faith that there is a force greater than myself directing the flow of my life.

I did not feel this faith in my thirties and forties. The agendas of life were too immediate, too important. My motivation to reach some unseen goal was too great. I used to believe that without the usual reactive displays of emotion, I would not feel a true connection in my life. Now I try to remember the daily practice of silent reflection and prayer. Silence tempers the fire and provides me with a deeper connection to the Mystery, and ultimately, to myself. Prayer opens my heart to the love that surrounds me and to the lives of all sentient beings.

My three children are grown, I have four beautiful grandchildren, and I have been married to a wonderful man for nearly ten years. Now that I have entered the age of the wise woman or "crone," I find it interesting that in the midst of all this vibrant life, I am spending more time with Death. Death lives in the Mystery. I watch its movement and

I am beginning to see my reflection in Death's eyes. I contemplate the moment when I am no longer breathing and I fall away from my physical body to truly join the energy of the Mystery. It is possible for youth to evade the reality of physical death, and I have chosen not to ignore it any longer. The paradox is that as I turn toward death I feel more vital and alive.

Finally, I believe that as we begin to feel welcomed into the Mystery we are taught to trust the contradictions that surround our lives. Living in the Mystery calls us to a deeper, more profound faith. It asks us to take action, be of service, love ourselves and others more, and it gently guides us into the awareness that we can trust that it is all right not to know.

J.T. O'Hara

Dog Walk

J.T. O'Hara is a renaissance woman. She is not only head of J.T. O'Hara and Associates, a book packaging firm (whose motto is "Frankly my dear, we do give a damn!"), but is also a painter, poet, songwriter, screenwriter, and published writer. (She is also an excellent dog walker.) Rob Morton of Morton Books referred to her in the New Yorker *as "the legendary salon keeper" of Beverly Hills. Invitations to her monthly Sunday afternoon salons are much sought after by westside literati and people in "the Business."*

J.T., who has lived in Beverly Hills since 1973, was born in New York, where she was taught to live by the eleventh commandment: "Thou shalt not give up." After she moved to California, she began to explore her love of painting (numerous celebrities are among her clients) and to indulge her love of the sea and sport fishing. She also was encouraged by friends to try her hand at writing. So for her second act, she became a writer. She recalls, "I wrote a book, Beep, *for Warner Books and a novella,* The Wings of the Magnificent Concubine *(which got me a great letter of rejection from Random House, which I framed and put on my wall)."*

She has been a fund-raiser for nonprofit organizations, and her third book, The Gift of Happiness Belongs to Those Who Unwrap It *(Andrews McMeel), was based on these experiences. She has also written* Are You Fit to Be Tied? *(questions for prospective mates), and has helped her dog Jiggs pen* Hound Wisdom, or How to Survive in a Dog-Sniff-Dog World.

I WATCH A SEAGULL ON HER WAY TO THE BEACH DANCE an abstract painting in the sky. I am on my early morning dog walk, the moment of pensive quietness we all need before we have to face the mechanical world.

I am blessed to have been the rescuer of an incredibly loyal new friend. The little dog had an abusive beginning and was left by the roadside, broken leg and all—a little tan Westie whose impishly innocent face stopped all the traffic.

After a few months of recuperation and getting to know each other, we now have our routine down to a science. One whistle from me and she is ready to go for our walk. This morning, as I put her leash on and pet her, I say, "It looks like an early-morning pea-soup alert."

The morning chill adds to the fog as we walk our regular beat. Watching the seagull dive in straight lines, then circle around point to point like a Jasper Johns, I think about my friend Joyce in New York. She has always been enchanted by paintings like that, with their reflections of the wonderful, jazzy, free, and crazy city of New York.

Then I remember a sign that David Puttnam had in his office when he was with Columbia Pictures. The saying was by Flaubert, and I loved it: "Be regular and ordinary in your life, like a bourgeois, so that you may be violent and original in your work." My father was my hero. He was a doctor, and during the war years he cared for and listened to his patients for only two dollars a visit.

There must be a balance between hunger for success and reaching out, I think, between doing for oneself and doing for others. I'm convinced that the true waste in our lives is to not use the power we have to motivate one another.

I've always tried to write my life story in the center of the page, not in the margins. There are many branches in a woman's life—wife, mother, creative being, friend, and so on. When one of the branches gets dry, it is time to amputate it and start growing another one.

For this reason, I decided long ago that I was going to laugh often, win the respect of intelligent people and the affection of children, appreciate beauty, find the best in others, and leave the world a little better than I found it. To know that even one life has breathed easier because I have lived—this, to me, will be my success.

I'm also thinking that we hold on to the past as a way of grounding ourselves, but rather than doing that, it instead weakens our ability to accept the moment. I like to think I hold on to the past only in close, quality friendships. I've always told my friends, "How do I count on thee? Let me love thy ways . . ." And they've always been there for me, both in my salad days and in my more challenging times.

The birds are so low now that, as I walk under the silent blanket of fog, I feel the air move as their wings brush near my face.

I meet a lovely Japanese woman who moves gracefully through the mist on her morning walk, and I notice she is carrying a crucifix in her hand. We exchange greetings, and she bends down to pet my dog, saying, "I've been thinking about past lives this morning. Maybe I was once a dog in a previous life. Maybe a sheepdog on an English estate, working the sheep. Do you think you've had a past life?"

"Well," I say, "I always try to see all people in a positive light. After all, I think my eyes are the eyes that God sees with."

Tears form in her eyes and she touches my hand. I want to remove her sadness, so I add, "Actually, in past lives I must have been Francis of Assisi and Eleanor of Aquitaine . . . only kinder and better looking."

We both laugh the best kind of laugh—a shared one. Then we continue off into the fog in different directions.

Sometimes we have to go inside ourselves to get more out of life. As her question suggested, that Japanese woman did just that. And my indisputable drug of choice is not "caffeine, first thing." It is optimism. With a dose of that once a day, how can I miss?

As I walk home slowly, I look down and see a shiny quarter in the grass. I feel so rich, so free, I do not bend to pick it up.

Carol Ann Curthoys

Laughter, Lost and Found

Carol Ann Curthoys is a retired college English and writing instructor. She lives in Tualatin, Oregon, and is an avid hiker, having hiked in Oregon, Washington, California, Ireland, and Austria. For the last few years, she has been tapping her creative energy directing a foundation that supports single mothers who are returning to school and children who show talent in the arts. These activities and her wonderful daughter, son, and friends keep her sane and happy. Writing has been a part of her life for most of her life and she always has a story to tell. She has been on a soul journey for several years and continues to work at discovering her truths.

IN THIS LAST THIRD OF MY LIFE, I HAVE FOUND MY laugh. Finding it was like finding a complete shell on the beach. It has been part revelation and part discovery, but always cathartic and joyous. Somewhere deep inside me now is the "knowing." Some call it wisdom. I call it my true self, which emerged from the depths of my soul, and, along with my laugh, keeps me balanced.

Many years of intense living before my true self emerged contributed to the disappearance of my laugh. A divorce that ended an almost quarter-century marriage, my children leaving home for college, returning to college myself for a master's degree, and a relationship that ended in an emotional crash all created a tension inside my soul that could not be relieved, or so it seemed.

In middle age, reworking my life as a single woman was exhausting, difficult, and time consuming. I was trying to discover my soul—the part of me that enjoyed me, my values, my beliefs, and to set goals that my soul could celebrate. I was on a journey to wholeness, to self-confidence, to self-determination. The journey sometimes led me down false paths. Each time, I retraced my steps, to begin again, walking more carefully and with greater focus.

I kept walking down my chosen road, kept believing that someday soon I would be at peace. And as the years passed, my heart began to heal, my feet began to dance, my brain began to work in ways that were pleasing to me, and my smile reappeared. Life filled the empty spaces with new friendships, new experiences, new relationships with my children, a new college degree, and new paths to trod.

But something was still missing.

Then, one day, I laughed, a full hearty laugh. I no longer remember what I laughed at, but it felt as if I were opening up like a butterfly's wings unfurling after it emerges from the confinement of the chrysalis. Next I felt as if I were filling up, the way ocean fills holes that children dig in the sand. And I knew. I knew that I had been missing my sense of humor. In my pursuit of happiness, I had forgotten how to laugh! I'm not talking about the ability to laugh at a joke or tell a funny story, but the ability to look at possibilities, to find the light where there seems to be darkness, and then to laugh at life with a giant outpouring of energy. Now, when my sense of humor is absent, I feel split into two parts. When laughter erupts from deep in my soul's well and encompasses me, I feel whole.

My sense of humor teaches me to appreciate the joys and, in turn, to try to appreciate the sadness, the pain. I know, now, how to play with the presence and focus of a child, yet be the adult teacher, when I care for a very special two-year-old. I know now the joy of honest sharing with friends, which often involves laughing heartily at myself. I know now how to hike a new trail with confidence that my body will get me not only to the top of the ridge, but back to the trailhead—from beginning to beginning, just as the beginning of my laugh brought the beginning of awareness of my true self.

I'm not saying I never laughed before. I did, at jokes, movies, TV sitcoms, and children's antics. But my new laugh is different. While my laugh was away, like me, it changed. Now it is deeper, richer, and louder, starting with a giggle, then rolling into a thunderous howl. When I'm the first one laughing, the rest of my companions are soon laughing too, and the laughter is like arms reaching out in hugs for each of us.

Sometimes my newly found laugh overwhelms me, and I weep as I roar out loud. The strength of it surprises me, since it seems to come from some unknown depth I've yet to explore. But even though my physical size has remained the same over the years, give or take a few pounds, the size of my soul and the depth of my knowledge have grown huge and are now unfolding and presenting themselves in my life.

Would this new me, this wisdom-filled true self, have emerged without the new laugh? Perhaps. You may say the acquisition of wisdom is inevitable with aging. Maybe. But this laughing, this roaring-out-loud, overwhelming laughing leaves me feeling more expanded and energized than I ever remember feeling before. This laugh keeps me in touch with my soul and loosens the words that flow easily from the depths of wisdom.

Since my laugh erupted from its hiding place, my life has also erupted. I created a foundation to help single mothers realize their goals and to support children with talent and desire in the arts. I have discovered the adventure in traveling to places I never dreamed I would go. And people! People appear. They come rolling in like the tide, just as my new laugh came rolling up from deep within my soul, to enrich, challenge, and fulfill my life. It is a constant source of joy to know that others are benefiting from my newfound self. I am grateful for the people who have been and are still in my life, even those who have been difficult or demeaning, because they teach me to stand in my integrity and be true to what I believe.

My sense of humor provides me with a way to look at life's happenings with an eye and ear to the upside. Without it, my soul would still feel split in two. I am also learning to trust my new self, which helps me find the balance I have so desperately needed. I choose my friends carefully, not haphazardly as I once did, and of course they have to be people with whom I can laugh. I confront problems not with fear, but with an examination of choices and fullness of heart.

The exhilaration I feel now is the same as when I take a long, muscle-throbbing hike to a viewpoint and look out over a range of mountain peaks. I know without a doubt that the life I've lived, with its pains, sorrows, and joys, has brought me to this pinnacle, to the realization of the authentic self I was meant to be. I am here because I kept moving forward, one step at a time, until I found laughter—full-throated, chest-expanding, from-the-heart laughter.

Carolyn Piper

What's the Big Deal?

Fifty-six years old, Carolyn Piper is a retired occupational therapist who lives in Vermont with her husband and two sons. When not writing, she can usually be found either in her large organic garden or busily at work at her sewing machine. Carolyn, who lost her hearing due to a childhood illness, has a cochlear implant, which has been of great help to her.

"SO, WHAT'S THE BIG DEAL?" ASKED AN OLD FRIEND with whom I had been out of contact for thirty years. Back then, you see, I was only hard of hearing, and managed to scrape along with lip reading and a lot of bluffing. Nowadays, I am totally deaf, and when my friend and I started e-mailing, I remarked again and again in my e-mails on the status of my hearing—finally provoking that question to rear its interesting head.

"Them there's fighting words" was my first thought when I saw his question on my screen, even though I knew that in the context of the conversation, which was Buddhist in nature and slanted toward karmic reckoning, no harm had been meant. Still, the challenge in the query brought me up short.

Now, I am one who tends to worry ideas as a dog gnaws a bone. I began to wonder: what, after all, *is* the big deal about being deaf in a hearing world? Or is there one? Am I making too much of my disability? If so, why? Realistically, figuring out what's the big deal about hearing loss isn't that difficult. Free and easy communication is the coin of the realm in our fast-paced world. Fitting in socially, vocationally, and emotionally without the ability to readily understand spoken speech is challenging, to say the least.

From a practical point of view, living with deafness is a very big deal indeed when a simple visit to the doctor can strike fear into your heart and mind. *Will I understand what is said? Will they understand me? Will I hear my name called in the waiting room? Will I misunderstand?* (This once happened to me, when I was told to get dressed and come out to the waiting room, and ended up instead staying in the exam room, actually falling asleep for two hours until I was discovered and rerouted back into my day's activities.) The questions—no matter how many times we have been in such situations—pound through our heads, keeping time with the rhythm of a fast-beating heart. This much is plain. Hearing people, no matter how good willed or caring, can little comprehend or understand how miscommunication affects us.

But why, I wondered, did I feel constrained with new acquaintances—as my old friend for all practical purposes was—to bring up these facts in an almost rhythmic repetition? Why does deafness resonate in my mind so strongly and so repetitively, when it would seem that a simple statement of fact would suffice?

Perhaps I and anyone else with a disability—whether physical, emotional, or mental—when faced with a new person or situation in our lives, are in a sense dealing once more with an old question we like to think is long buried, but which in reality we never did resolve: *Will I be accepted and liked as I was before I became disabled?*

And so we push it out front, waiting and watching to see what the reaction will be, processing once more the implications of our deficit. We hope against hope that it will make no difference, knowing that too often it makes a very big difference in how people both perceive and treat us.

Of course, there is more to it than that. Like most people who have gone deaf in adulthood, I spent a long time wandering in the land of denial. For a long and very painful time, I refused to accept my new world, dreading that each encounter would unmask me as a refugee from normal society—one of "them" instead of one of "us." Only gradually did I learn to integrate my loss of hearing into a new self, where it is all right simply to be myself.

As Carl Jung said following his mourning the loss of his wife, "It cost me a great deal to regain my footing. Now I am free to become who I really am." Just so. In fact, so heavy can be the price of denial, that some of us begin to overcompensate—pushing the fact of our loss relentlessly ahead of us, lest we lose sight of it. In doing so, we forget once more our own humanity and sense of belonging. We are afraid, as I know I am, that if we do not keep constant vigil, we will lapse into pretending once more, and be swept away and drowned in a renewed tide of denial.

And so I repeat, "I am deaf, I am deaf, I am deaf." A person who has never had to meet and adjust to a physical challenge might well be excused for becoming both bored and exasperated by such repetition. And, despite Buddhist philosophy, perhaps it was so with my old/new friend, whose question threw into stark relief a habit that may well have been painfully apparent to those around me, but which I myself had been unaware.

Acknowledging and accepting a disability of any sort is necessary if we are to master our lives. Dwelling on them past the point of their relevance to any particular person or situation, I have now learned, is not. Still, there is another side to this coin. While there are undoubtedly times when we may lose our balance and inappropriately emphasize our losses at the expense of our total selves, there is also no doubt that my deafness—or your disability—is indeed a very big deal in life in ways that are also appropriate, positive, and often overlooked.

It is the nature of life that one thing or another will go wrong for most of us sooner or later. Lives and hearts are injured or broken, and we must learn to go on, healing as we go, reinventing ourselves along the way. But if we are paying attention, if we are willing to live consciously as we meet our challenges, we can learn to sing again and, in ways that we might not have dreamed possible, actually be born anew.

I once asked a fellow member of ALDA (The Association of Late Deafened Adults) how deafness had changed him. His response describes perfectly the sunny side of losses and big deals in our lives. "Without my losses," he replied, "I would still be the same small-minded chauvinistic idiot I was before."

So, what's the big deal? Like everything else in life, the question turns out to have two sides. Yin and yang. Negative and positive. Learning to tell the difference, learning to balance the pluses and minuses a disability brings to our lives is the challenge. And it is in the meeting of challenges and opening of our hearts and minds to new questions that we may find ourselves face to face with the biggest deal of all—learning to grow and sing the song of life to new melodies.

Saundra Thurman-Custis

Two Tons of Metal or a Balanced Account

Saundra Thurman-Custis is a devoted wife, mother of two, and grand-mother of two. She lives in Bowie, Maryland, with her husband of twenty-six years. To describe the degrees she has earned, the awards she has been awarded, or the successful business enterprise she launched would not tell you who she is. To meet her family is to know her. They are her legacy. Laughter and joy in her home are symbols of her wealth and prosperity.

NOW I KNOW YOU'VE HEARD ABOUT THE VICISSITUDES of competing with the other woman. Now we're even hearing more about competing with the other man. That's right, my best girlfriend lost her husband to a man. How do you respond to some mess like that? Since that was a new one on me, I just threw her a big party and celebrated the fact that she was moving on to what had to be up. Friends brought the frilliest of lingerie and most expensive fragrances and cremes from Victoria's Secrets. We wanted to reassure her that she was still "all that" and she needed to evaluate her assets and get on with this gift called life.

How much time had she wasted trying to figure out what was "wrong with her"? We had spent countless hours playing psychologist because "He doesn't seem to be interested anymore." But life truly is too short to deal with OPP (other people's problems). Well, hallelujah, and slap me blind, he figured out on his own what sexual position he preferred. So let it go, and pass the Asti Spumanti.

Desiring to be a supportive wife, my friend had left law school when her husband decided he wanted to return to graduate school full-time. She had been an excellent student, had made law review, and had been identified by the dean as one of the school's most promising students. With much uncertainty, she had followed her husband to the university *of his choice*. She had subjugated her aspirations and accomplishments to her husband's desires. Now, two years later, she found herself alone, with a small child, and with major decisions to make.

After everyone left the party, she thanked me. The time spent with friends who really cared provided the emotional lift she needed. Then she started talking about how afraid she was to pick up the pieces and begin again. I just let her take all the time she needed to think out loud and listen to what was in her head. Then I asked her what she really wanted to do. She said she wanted to become a lawyer but had decided that returning to law school now would be impossible.

She explained the number of classes she would have to complete and the time needed to prepare to practice law. She finally exclaimed, "I would be forty years old before I started my career!" I filled her glass with her favorite wine and responded, "You're going to be forty anyway; why not be a forty-year-old lawyer?"

With that affirmation and a belief in herself, she set out to accomplish just that. With much difficulty and many setbacks, she achieved her goal. I attended her graduation and she went on to specialize in practicing law for the disabled. She excelled in her career, she was walking in her gift, and she inspired everyone around her.

My grandmother once told me that the greatest sin is to betray who we are. She believed that God has planted within each of us a unique gift. We have to find and develop that gift to make our contribution on this earth. No other person can contribute that gift to mankind with the same effect. When we fail to nurture and develop our gift, we are actually betraying ourselves.

I learned long ago that my gift was in the area of creative art. Early in life, my writing brought joy to others. I enjoy stirring up thoughts that lay dormant in people whose lives had become mundane. I like interweaving various schools of thought and disciplines to provoke the reader to new insights about an issue or subject.

Writing gave me a lot of pleasure, stretched me, and began to mold me into the unique person I was designed to be. Although I derived a great deal of gratification from writing, I pursued it only as an avocation. I met and married a wonderful man. We have been married now over twenty-five years and have two beautiful, talented, and gifted children. Our growing family required more and more of my time and attention. It was not unusual for me to work a ten- or twelve-hour day. I seemed to give more love, patience and understanding than I received.

Now you can't withdraw funds from the bank that have not been deposited, without getting back a notice. I had received several notices that I was overdrawing my personal account over the years, and I did what I could to try to keep a balance, but recently I got my final notice, the one that moved me to act.

It came the week I awoke to the fact that, after all these years of long-suffering and sacrifice for the benefit of marriage and family, my husband seemed to pay more attention to his car than he did to me. *I'm competing with my husband's ride.* The other day I found myself thinking that if I have another life to live, I might be better off coming back as my husband's Volvo. I would surely get more loving, more attention, even more compassion, if I were that two tons of metal sitting in the driveway.

The day I received my final notice I was sitting in my kitchen. This was on a Sunday, so I certainly didn't sit down until I had finished preparing Sunday dinner, and, mind you, I cook his meals just the way his momma cooks for him. She has the meat cut specifically for the menu. You know, when she is preparing pork chops, she has the butcher cut pockets inside so she can stuff them with her special dressing. We're not going to talk about all the extra cookware needed to prepare the homemade sauces and desserts he's so fond of. I let my homemade rolls rise twice, so you know preparing Sunday dinner is a commitment for me.

While dinner was cooking, I washed and folded a week's worth of laundry. Heaven forbid if the laundry isn't Blue Cheer clean and the whites aren't Clorox white and Downy soft. How could he possibly strut around all those smiling faces at church, or waltz around those big shots perpetrating on Capitol Hill if little wifey didn't take care of business at the home place?

All this homemaking and working to help support the family didn't leave much time for writing, but I thought I was doing what I had to do. In reality, I wasn't living, I was just accepting whatever life handed me. What had I done with my unique gift of writing? It was buried somewhere, and I was making all kinds of excuses to myself for not unearthing it and developing it. I had betrayed my gift. I had committed the great sin my grandmother had cautioned me about.

Let me get back to the day I got my final notice. My husband came rushing in, obviously very disturbed about something. Abruptly interrupting my concentration on beating those egg whites for a perfect meringue, he frantically announced, "I noticed some little spots all over my car after I had it washed at the [touchless] carwash. When I talked with the guy, he claimed he didn't know what the spots were or what could have caused them." I knew he was furious, because of the furrow that had formed on his forehead.

Well he didn't waste any time resolving the issue: he decided to wash and wax the car himself. He headed straight to the garage with all due and deliberate speed, as in Monopoly when the direction is "Do Not Pass Go." He got his lambs wool and Turtle Wax, popped some smooth jazz in the portable CD player, and got straight down to business.

Yes indeed, that was the day I got my notice and started living again. I propped my big butt up on this here kitchen stool and watched that man rub and polish that car of his until it had a luster so deep that Turtle Wax could have used the picture to increase sales fourfold. I'm not sure the shine looked that good the day he brought it home. He applied and reapplied the wax so meticulously, and polished and buffed so thoroughly you needed sunglasses to get a peek at that car. I sat watching him for more than an hour, trying to figure out where he got all the energy to manually massage that car. I watched him get down on his knees and shine those tires. When he finished I could see the light bouncing off all four tires, and the shine on the chrome was blinding. I'm telling you, every inch of that ride got his personal undivided attention.

He bent, stretched, and twisted his upper torso over every inch of the vehicle. His body was contorted in ways I have never experienced. I said to myself, it sure would be nice to have all that action going on in here sometime. Now, just the night before, he was too tired to do his real business, or, let's say, finish it.

Now if he took care of me with all that urgency and attentiveness I would be one satisfied woman. People would stop me on the street and ask what happened. My grin would be so wide, people would swear I was on something. My eyes would be so bright the addicts would be asking for my contact.

All those years of marriage, I just kept giving of myself without getting back enough attention and appreciation to keep my account balanced. It was quite a revelation to see my husband give so much to a car, just two tons of metal. However you describe it, in the final analysis, that car is a depreciating asset.

Now remember, this was still Sunday. After he was done, we sat down to dinner at our dining room table, which was dressed with white linen, our best crystal, silver candlesticks, and a vase filled with roses from my garden. While savoring his dinner, my husband let me know that he was not going in to the office on Monday. Since I'm an eternal optimist, I'm thinking we're going to stay up late and enjoy one another, or he'll get up early and prepare breakfast for me, or, at the least, he'll bring me a cup of fresh coffee and we'll linger in the afterglow of uninhibited passion.

What was I thinking? On Monday morning, he got up earlier than usual to take that car to the dealership; said he had heard something unusual, so the car needed some adjusting and tuning. Don't get me started on how much tuning I needed. Right about then I would have settled on one of those Jiffy Lube discount specials to get some relief. What was going on in his head that he was not attentive to something unusual about me?

Now just how does one compete with two tons of metal, the other woman, the other man, or anything else? Well, here's my advice—*you don't.*

When you get that notice that your account is overdrawn, take your reality check. You need to *recognize* that you alone are responsible for balance in your life. Remember your unique gift. Even when life demands that you put it on hold, you must never relinquish, subjugate, or totally betray it. If you do, you betray yourself, you betray who you are, the real you.

When you find yourself unfulfilled, understand that you're only at a turning point. Nurture and develop your gift, get your life back in balance, and determine to maintain that balance for a fulfilled and enjoyable life. You don't compete with anything or anyone outside of yourself. You strive to become the best you can be.

Life will respond to your active pursuit of your special gift. The operative word here is "active." Time waits for no one. Life seeks a balance, and you alone are responsible for a balanced and fulfilled life.

Well, my husband got the spots off his car and I got my reality check, my final notice. Suffice it to say that we eat Sunday dinners out so that I have more time for writing. I'm off to meet with my agent. She's negotiating my most recent book deal. The interested party wants both publishing and movie rights. I'm getting it together for me, and I know at the end of this journey, I'll say, "Well done."

Billie Biederman

Relieved

Billie Biederman attributes her varied interests, some of her passions, and her network of eclectic friends to her Gemini nature, which draws her to the young, the old, the spiritual, the creative, the unusual, and the ordinary. She enjoys books, films, theater, and long telephone visits; and loves to read and write.

She graduated from Seward Park High School, where she now serves on the board of its alumni association. She enhanced her education by working in not-that-many jobs, most in her native New York and some in California, where she lived for three years in her twenties, working for comedy writers—which almost cost her her sense of humor.

Billie can't remember when she didn't write. Her earliest serious efforts, published in a community center newsletter for servicemen during World War II, grew into a 10,000-word monthly column, which she wrote for four years until the war ended. Eleven of her essays were published in the company newspaper.

*She lays claim to a loaded computer of work in progress and intends
to spend the rest of her life completing as many as she can manage. Given
that Gemini nature, she will inevitably be distracted and stop to smell a
flower or two along the way.*

"HOW DOES IT FEEL TO BE SIXTY?"

When I asked the question of my teacher at the Gurdjieff Foundation, she took her time to ponder it before answering. Her admir-
ing students were making merry, enjoying the occasion of her
landmark birthday in her home, where we gathered for the evening's
festivities. The atmosphere was a vivid contrast to our weekly meetings at the Foundation, where a group of us sat, almost primly in a
circle, directing our questions and observations to her when we
had the courage to speak. She was extraordinarily intelligent and
learned, no small requirement to guide our studies of the teachings
of the Eastern mystic G. Gurdjieff and his followers. The fun side of
our teacher was not even hinted at during our weekly meetings, so at
this celebration, I, who had no social impediments, experienced an
unaccustomed shyness and awkwardness in her presence. The party
was a rare switch of ambiance, a 180-degree turn from our usual
solemn discussions.

The punch had been pleasantly spiked, helping to ease the anxieties of some of us awestruck students; and music, conversation, and
funny stories helped us cross the line to informality. Those students not
privy to a social relationship with her were confused and delighted to
see our erudite teacher thoroughly enjoying her birthday party like any
ordinary person.

Wanting to appear lighthearted yet thoughtful, I asked her how it
felt to be sixty—a number quite remote from my own reality at the
time. As she prepared to answer, the other students, ever eager to sip

from her fount of wisdom, gathered 'round. We had learned that she listened in a special, deeply thoughtful way, and responded accordingly.

At last she uttered one succinct word: "Relieved."

I blinked.

"I am relieved to be sixty."

She went on, "You know, when we are very young, we are in such a hurry to be grown up. We are filled with anxiety and impatience to go hither and yon, to do this and that, to make money, to succeed, and so forth."

Hearing her speak, in her mildly pontifical way, the merrymakers quieted and rallied to catch every nugget of her wisdom.

"In our teens and twenties, we are absorbed in educating ourselves and plotting our futures; then we are busy working toward realizing our dreams and ambitions, which takes years of hard work. We want things and are driven to strive, to accumulate, to succeed. We become involved in business or raising families or in trying to save the world in some way. It goes on for a very long time."

She paused, allowing us to inscribe her words on our mental slates, to absorb her overview of life. In the quiet, I reflected on my own ambitions to do better, to travel and see more of the world, as she had, to leap the barriers that limitations of money and education had put in my path. She had done so much and knew so much and, being still vital, would do so much more.

"But why 'relieved'?" I asked.

"Because at sixty it all falls away. I don't *have* to do or go or prove anything else. The need for all that striving stops—falls away." She shrugged as if to demonstrate her point.

Although puzzled, I nodded. I tacitly understood that she was imparting something profound, but a small, rebellious member of my collective personality resisted her answer. Gurdjieff himself had said that everything we hear or read is only theory—until it becomes our own experience. I would have to wait.

Years later, when I turned sixty, I don't remember being "relieved." Given our different scenarios, there had to be different answers from the one given by my teacher years before. I had not married or borne children; I did not have a comfortable financial status I could take for granted; I did not have formal higher education to provide me with a career ladder to climb. Yet I had managed to make a modest, decent living and create an interesting life. If one's activities and friends are useful barometers, I could be considered a mild success.

At sixty, I was working at my last full-time job and enjoying my independence. I was far from letting go of life or feeling relieved. With friends and family all over the globe who wanted visiting, I did a bit of traveling, not to every exotic spot on the planet, but to enough places to make for several good chapters in my memory book. I held fast to my dream of being published. Having given myself enough goals and wanting more from life than most people I know, I didn't see any "relief" in sight.

Reaching sixty did not change me, nor did I allow the number to sentence me to being an old woman or alter the direction or pace of my life. The subject of age is a private matter, to be revealed when necessary for something official or for the fun of it, but otherwise, at my own discretion. The man I worked for did not know for nine years that I was twelve years his senior. When he found out, he remained discreet. Exercising great wisdom, he did not treat me any differently— well, perhaps with a tad more respect and a touch of awe. My job was not in jeopardy as far as I could tell.

On the odd occasion when asked my age, I invite the curious to guess. My standard answer to any number offered has usually been "That's close enough." It fills me with glee when the mark is missed by a mile, or even a yard. Most of the "guessers" shave as much as fifteen years off my actual number. About that, I could admit to being "relieved," but "pleased" is the better word!

After passing sixty, it is inevitable to think about certain things differently, but one's basic nature endures. Injustice anywhere in the world and laxity in high places still stir my passions and make me reach for the boxing gloves and my sword—in the shape of a pen. The fury I feel when the vulnerables of the world (the very young and the very old) are abused or left defenseless turns my vision scarlet. Even though the larger issues—which surely cannot be cured by a modest donation check from me—often discourage and overwhelm me, I do what I can.

At sixty, I did begin to let certain things go. Great passions require great energy; life on the battlements calls for discernment about which enemies to take on. Although relinquishing a little independence and accepting help, when offered, is self-preserving and not necessarily weak, such changes take getting used to. In *It's Better to Be over the Hill than under It*, Eda LeShan writes that she had been shocked to realize that people who talked about old people were talking about her. Once past the jolt of reality, however, one can claim the benefits, and the triumph of getting there.

Perks that accrue to seniors are decidedly satisfying and to be relished: half fares on public transit; discounts dispensed by airlines, hotels, and other establishments; lower-priced movie tickets: all provide a comforting sense of victory (and a touch of entitlement) to the mature citizen. Whatever the rewards and privileges, I claim them all. And arriving at a certain age allows one to be "feisty." Another plus. Being thought eccentric has been one of my aspirations; I hope I am showing signs of it.

One risk, however, is to lose contact with the younger generation. To my great relief and joy, the companionship of younger people is still one of life's gifts to me. I am surprised and flattered when they ask my advice or opinion. The generation gap disappears when fused by mutual respect. Never mind what I can teach the young; I am interested in what they can teach *me*. This point of view was hatched from one of my mother's many wise utterances: "One could live to be a hundred and still die a fool."

Another was brought to me by a long-forgotten friend from an ashram in India: "Every man is my teacher." We can even learn from those whose very ignorance shows us how we would wish *not* to be. The guru did not say that every *old* man is my teacher— just every man (and I assume every woman). I would further amend it to include every young person, and even every child, as significant contributors to my ongoing education.

Life is indeed a banquet and I have not gone hungry yet. It keeps me busy with the mundane and surprises me with the unexpected; my interest and attention are regularly captured by invitations, celebrations, greetings, and farewells. I sip at the fountain and nibble at the feast, even as I see others starving themselves. I am baffled by people who are bored or claim they have nothing to do; I have little patience for their complaints, especially those in good physical health and with an abundance of resources.

My mother observed that if everybody formed a circle and threw their troubles into the middle, after looking around at some of the others, they would gladly snatch their own back and say no more.

One of my closest friends is immobilized by polio and other physical problems, yet runs a household from a hospital bed. Her room holds two oxygen tanks, a respirator, and a suctioning machine; a tracheotomy tube in her throat helps her breathe. Her speech was once cut off for three months, yet she managed to communicate with friends all over the world; she writes wonderful notes and letters and heartwarming essays that celebrate her happy childhood and her family. Her paintings, collages, photographs, trinkets, and loving gifts decorate every wall and bookshelf; she gives dimension to the words *life* and *spirit*, and continues to raise my consciousness about what matters and what doesn't.

What I am relieved about is that I am still alive; in good health; and very much interested in life's challenges, rewards, and surprises. To ask, "What am I supposed to learn from this?" instead of, "Why me?" is to die less a fool.

The Now is where it is and where I am. It is written somewhere that yesterday is memory, tomorrow is imagination, and today is a gift, which is why it is called the present. Oh yes, it is good to have memories and it is fun to plan, but to have this moment—at any age—is to have it all.

At seventy-seven, to be sure, some things have fallen away, but to believe that "the best is yet to come" is, well, yes, a relief.

Mary Trimble

———— ◊ ————

Live Your Dream

Mary Trimble is a freelance writer who lives with her husband on Camano Island, Washington. In her writing, she draws on personal experiences, including being a purser and ship's diver aboard the tall ship M.S. Explorer, *a Peace Corps volunteer in west Africa, and a traveler on both a 13,000-mile South Pacific cruise aboard the* Impunity *and on extensive RV trips. Mary is active with the American Red Cross and has responded to several local and national disasters.*

Her 350-plus articles have appeared in magazines including Writer's Digest, Coast to Coast, RV Life, Get Up & Go!, Family Motor Coaching, Sail, Waterfront, RV West, RV Today, The Rotarian, Manufactured Homes, Western RV News, Alpaca Magazine, American Livestock, *and* Trailblazer.

Her young-adult novel, Rosemount, *with settings in eastern Washington and Oregon, was published in 2000.* Rosemount's *sequel,* McClellan's Bluff, *is due to be published in 2002, also by Atlantic*

Bridge Publishing. She is a member of Women Writing the West, Society of Children's Book Writers and Illustrators, Electronically Published Internet Connection, and Pacific Northwest Writers Association.

ELEANOR ROOSEVELT ONCE SAID, "THE FUTURE BELONGS to those who believe in the beauty of their dreams." Dreams allow us to see ourselves in a different light, imaging or visualizing ourselves out of our current status and into a more desirable one.

You *can* live your dream. Let's look at some ways you can make it happen.

First of all, look at your dream realistically. Is it something you really want to do? Are you willing to make sacrifices to make it happen? Will it be in your best interest to have this dream fulfilled? Pretend it has already happened. Although we can't always visualize just how a fulfilled dream will be, we can come close. Be realistic—drop the romance, the rosy glow that usually accompanies dreams. Acknowledge the tough times. Does it fit? Can you see yourself there? Is your dream worth the tough times? If so, see yourself overcoming obstacles.

I don't know what your dreams are, but I can share with you some of the dreams my husband Bruce and I have had, and tell you how we made them happen.

Bruce and I love adventure. In 1979, after we'd been married a year, we yearned to do something different. What about the Peace Corps? I can't remember a time when I hadn't dreamed of seeing Africa. We learned that as Peace Corps volunteers we could fulfill this dream and, at the same time, help meet desperate needs in a tiny west African country, The Gambia.

In order to make our Africa dream happen, we had to sacrifice. We both gave up good jobs. (Peace Corps volunteers receive no salary, just a modest living-expense allowance.) Living in an African Mandinka village 250 miles from the capital city, Banjul, and 150 miles from the nearest paved road was fascinating, but it wasn't easy. Our home was a mud-brick hut with a grass-thatched roof. Temperatures soared to 115 degrees. We drew our water from a United Nations well, thankful that it was pure. Our shared latrine was a hole in the ground, surrounded by a flimsy fence in a corner of the compound. We had no car, and I walked one mile to work. Fortunately for my husband, we lived next door to where he worked. Shopping for groceries at the open-air market entailed walking almost two miles.

Bruce worked with a United Nations well-digging unit, supplying much-needed deep wells for villages where wells were drying up during a long drought. As a health volunteer, I reported to work at a bush hospital, a thirty-two-bed facility that also housed well-baby and antenatal clinics. I was the only non-African at the hospital.

At first I cringed at this medical center, which appeared to be so unsanitary. Due to fuel shortages, we were often without electricity or running water. Flies were everywhere. Food for patients was prepared in large kettles cooked over open fires on the ground. Laundry was done by hand. But eventually I could see that we were accomplishing something. Lives were being saved and, through inoculations, diseases controlled.

Before my arrival, I had only heard of many of the illnesses commonly seen in The Gambia, such as polio, tuberculosis, and leprosy. In addition, I witnessed deaths caused by tetanus, snake bite, and countless cases of horrible skin diseases and infections. Still, the majority of deaths were the result of waterborne illnesses, especially among the very young and the old.

For two tough years we served in The Gambia, a time when we gained a profound awareness of life at a basic level. To trim away all the extras and live a plain, simple life was to learn new truths about our-selves. We were tougher than we ever imagined we could be.

We both believe we made a contribution in our host African coun-try, but it didn't compare with what we brought home—lasting mem-ories, feelings of accomplishment, and dreams fulfilled.

Back home, my husband began work in the marine electronic field. I attended college, earning an associate degree in computer sci-ence, which led to a job at a large insurance company as a program-mer analyst.

Eight years later, the bug struck again. This time, my husband's dream was calling to be fulfilled. He had always wanted to own a sail-boat—a real, ocean-going vessel—and circumnavigate the world. This dream was expensive. Not only would we not have incomes, but as anyone who has owned a boat knows, a boat is a hole in the water into which you throw money. We formed a five-year plan and worked toward our goal. Surprisingly, in two years we could see our way clear to set sail on a two-year trip.

Again, we sacrificed. We found a used sailboat, a forty-foot Bristol, and began to outfit it for ocean cruising. We altered the dream by agreeing on a more realistic South Pacific cruise that would allow us to sail at a more leisurely pace and stay longer at each port of call.

To prepare, we rarely bought anything not directly related to the cruise—no unnecessary clothes, no expensive trips, no major home improvements. We stocked up on a two-year food supply. We held a garage sale, eliminating extra stuff we'd accumulated. Since we didn't want the worry associated with renting our home, we sold it. This was traumatic for me, but our focus was our dream and that's what it took to get it done.

We lived on our boat for six months before departure, taking short, local trips, before departing on our 13,000-mile journey. Cruising, while it certainly holds its glorious moments, can also be demanding, dangerous, and exhausting. But the landfalls make it all worthwhile—to feel and smell the warm tropical air of Bora Bora, to see blue pristine water in Tahiti, to dive among the underwater coral gardens in the Kingdom of Tonga, and to make new friends everywhere among the warm, friendly people of the South Pacific. Another dream fulfilled.

When we returned, Bruce reentered the marine electronic field, but I had a new dream: becoming a professional writer. I began writing and submitting articles to magazines. Several months passed and, although I'd submitted articles to many magazines, I had no luck in getting published, only in collecting a discouraging pile of rejection slips.

I asked myself, "Is writing what I'm supposed to be doing?" I seemed to be taking the necessary steps. I spent all my spare time at my computer. Though I did meet family commitments, I usually turned down most activities that didn't point toward fulfilling a writer's dream—being published. Still, no success.

I prayed for a sign that I was on the right track. "Please," I prayed, "give me some sort of sign that I'm pointed in the right direction." Then, in one month, three different magazines published my work! I took that as a positive sign. Since then, I've had nearly 350 articles and one book published.

I still dream of doing exciting things. One way I satisfy that dream is by volunteering for the American Red Cross, locally and nationally. So far I've responded to several disasters and have been able to help victims of fires, hurricanes, mud slides, floods, and tornadoes. After the September 11, 2001, terrorist attacks in New York and Washington, D.C., I was sent to both areas to help families affected by this tragedy.

How do you know if your dream is worthy of the work it takes to turn it into reality? One sign is that if it's all uphill, if things eventually

don't fall into place, take a second look. Maybe you're dreaming someone else's dream. Or, maybe this dream needs to happen at another
time in your life. If your dream becomes a struggle, and that struggle
makes you unhappy, regroup and pray for guidance.

How do you make dreams happen?

Stay out of debt. Use credit only for absolute necessities, such as a
house mortgage. Debts control your life. Make the sacrifices necessary
to keep out of debt. You'll find a wonderful freedom.

Let go. Let go of the trappings often associated with success, like
a fancier car, home, or furnishings. Acquiring possessions is all right
if that's all you want out of life. But if you want to fulfill a dream, let
go of the extras.

Get rid of clutter. Look around your home and garage—boats,
trailers, motorcycles, quads, children's playground equipment, outdated
clothes, old books and magazines—how much of that stuff are you
using today? Clutter clogs up garages, basements, our thoughts, and our
lives. When we returned from the South Pacific, we sold our boat and
bought a home. Some of our friends were aghast: "How can you part
with that boat?" We could because we no longer needed it. Marinas are
full of boats that never go anywhere. Because at one time the boats
were important, people can't bear to part with them, and as a result
they use precious time on upkeep and pay expensive marina fees
on something that's become a burden, cluttering up their lives with
yesterday's dreams. Or, perhaps those boats are tomorrow's dreams that
never seem to get past the talking stage.

Simplify your life. Learn to savor simple foods. Reduce your
wardrobe. Enjoy long walks. My husband and I have found that most
of our dreams have been planned on our daily three-mile walks. Limit
activities to those you enjoy. Eliminate parties you really don't want to
attend or being with people you would just as soon not see.

Make yourself available for opportunity. In order to fulfill a dream, you must be ready. You never know how a dream's realization will manifest itself. If we shackle ourselves with nonessentials, we're likely to pass up opportunities that eventually will open doors to our dreams.

Take action. Go beyond the planning stage. Take steps to make your dream happen: take classes, attend lectures, talk to people who share your interests. Set the stage for your dream to take shape. It is easier to steer a moving car than one that's standing still.

Remember, though, to live for today. Having dreams and working toward them is good, but living is a present state—not the future and not the past. Find ways to enjoy life now, while working toward the future.

Take care of yourself. A simple lifestyle is a healthier way to live. Many issues I've mentioned here help keep us centered and free from unhealthful mental clutter and anxiety.

Pray for guidance. Is this the right goal at this time in your life? Ask for help in recognizing opportunities and overcoming obstacles.

Go for it. In my father's basement workshop hung a small plaque with words written by the eighteenth century British lexicographer and author Dr. Samuel Johnson: "Nothing will ever be attempted if all possible objections must be first overcome." Don't wait until everything is perfect before you act. Some obstacles can be ironed out as they occur and many of the problems we anticipate never happen. So, when most circumstances point toward success, make your move. Go for it.

Gail Balden

Ordinary Moments

*Gail Balden is founder and director of Creative Journeys Writing
Workshops for Women, an organization on the Oregon coast, designed
to bring women together to nurture their creative spirits and tell their
stories. In midlife, Gail has focused her energy on that which brings her
joy and meaning. Her desire is to help other women realize their life's
wisdom and reclaim their creative spirit and passion through the telling
of their stories.*

*Often a speaker for women's groups and spiritual retreats, she is also
a visual artist and freelance writer for magazines, newspapers, and liter-
ary journals. Her essay, "Your Life in Two Words," was published in
Beyond Words Publishing's* Our Turn, Our Time, *an anthology of
women telling how they have chosen to celebrate the second half of life.
Since turning fifty, Gail has taken a backpacking/canoeing Outward
Bound trip, bicycled across her home state of Michigan four times, climbed
Mt. St. Helen's, and become a certified sailor. She directs stage plays at*

the Coaster Theater Playhouse in Cannon Beach, Oregon. Her Web site address is www.creativejourneys.net.

SOME MOMENTS IN LIFE SEEM ETCHED IN MEMORY like a handprint in cement, where they remain unchanged and solid, a reminder mirrored in some simple act that life is sweet. Like that day over twenty-five years ago, a sunny day in the Southwest, as almost all days are. It may have been spring, my favorite time in the desert when, after refreshing rains, new life springs forth from the dryness.

I was cooking dinner for the family, probably something like spaghetti. My husband was cutting my daughter's hair, and her younger brother was playing on the floor with his toys, the kittens dancing about him. As I looked upon the scene while stirring the fragrant sauce on the stove, I noticed the light flowing through the large patio window, beyond which lay the fish pond we had built. It was our oasis in the desert, with its small waterfall. The pond in which my son had tried to catch koi with a stick, a string, and a safety pin, the pond where we thought the ducks we brought home would placidly swim and float, but who tore out all the water plants.

I saw my daughter sitting on the dining room chair, swathed in a pink plastic cape, her father gently combing and cutting her blond hair, the click of the scissors surprisingly soothing to me. I listened to their murmurings, punctuated at times by her laughter over something he said. My son was making truck noises, roaring and chugging, as he pushed his toy cars and trucks over the carpet, dodging the kittens. I felt a sense of quiet contentment as I looked at all of us and recognized it as happiness. This is it, I thought, this moment in an ordinary family, doing ordinary things.

Happiness. We wander about searching for this elusive quality that makes life worthwhile, yet it's seemingly always beyond our grasp. In

The Art of Happiness, His Holiness, the Dalai Lama says, "Your state of mind is key" in order to enjoy a happy and fulfilled life. I strive to remember this: my state of mind is key. But I live in the real world, and I agree with M. Scott Peck's opening line in *The Road Less Traveled*, "Life is difficult." People get sick, they lose their jobs, they struggle with the problems of daily life. And eventually we all die.

Keeping a light heart while trying to weave through the circumstances of life is one of our greatest challenges. A fine line to navigate, this life divided between joy and sorrow. The task, I think, is to find ways to discover those however-brief intervals of happiness within the layers of life, to open our eyes and really see that it is the simple things, those moments when some ordinary act reveals to us the essential nature and sweetness of life. Simple things like a blossom shower described to me by a friend whose husband was terminally ill. Immersed in a life of blood counts and transfusions, she remembers happily a soft Sunday afternoon when they sat beneath a marvelous tree filled with chartreuse-throated blossoms that gently floated down upon them as they ate oatmeal-raisin cookies and drank iced tea.

One such ordinary moment warms me like a soft cloak around my shoulders on a cold night. It is the time I held my young son on my lap in church, knowing this was probably one of the last times he would feel comfortable being the child on his mother's lap. He was growing up and moving away from me, as all youngsters do. I remember cherishing the moment, smelling the sweetness of his freshly washed hair, running my fingers through the corn silk of it, holding him close, the moment made all the more precious because I knew the time was coming when this, too, would be but a memory carried in my heart.

There was another moment just this year when I returned to the Midwest to see my father, my only remaining parent, for what was probably going to be the last time. After ninety-five years of life, time was ebbing for him. He had very little energy for anything except looking at the birds outside his window, so I took him a bird feeder. I went out the back door of the nursing home where he had come to be cared for at the end of his life. I walked around to the outside of his window and thrust the stake into the ground and hung the bell-shaped feeder from it. As I stood outside his window with the feeder, watching through the glass for a sign from my father as to whether this was the right location, or maybe a little left, a little right, I was keenly aware of the moment and how we were just father and daughter that day, as we were fifty years ago when we went to Farmer Grant's to pick strawberries on a Saturday morning, my first paying job from my father at a nickel a quart. Or like we were years ago on those rare Sunday mornings when I played hooky from Sunday School and we went fishing on Crooked Lake, nestled at the foot of a field of buttercups.

On this sunny spring day in Michigan, beneath a sky the color of a robin's egg, my father and I were just trying to decide where to place the bird feeder. We were not staring into the eyes of death just then. We were simply waiting for birds to come to us, to sing us their songs.

As a woman of fifty-eight, in what I consider to be the autumn of my life, I search for some bit of wisdom I can pass along, and this is it: happiness isn't something so big and unattainable and out there somewhere, just beyond our grasp. It isn't something we have to strive to reach or work hard to get or travel great distances to find. It doesn't even require large amounts of wealth or material possessions. It's right here, in this very instant of life, if we can only open our hearts to experience it and trust that it is as it should be.

I once believed if I followed all the rules and did the right thing, I would be rewarded with a good life. Experience has taught me differently, however, and I know there are no guarantees. By the age of thirty-three, I had already experienced my own chronic illness, hospitalizations, and surgeries; the murders of one of my students and my best friend; and my mother's unexpected death. I was no stranger to grief and loss. And even that happy family life with my husband and children, so sweet in my memory, one day began to unravel like a hem with weakened thread, changing our lives forever and leaving scars on our hearts. Sometimes it seems as if that is all that life's about—loss.

Yet, isn't it the pain that seasons and strengthens our souls? Do we really expect the road to be smooth, with no bumps? Or are we willing to admit that it is the very bumps that have made us who we are, those moments that test us and teach us our strength? This past year of my life has been harder than most, and brought me more sorrow. But the paradox is that joys are interwoven in the layers alongside the fragments of sadness.

Following my own advice and listening to my intuition, I decided, at age fifty-eight, to live the quote, "Leap and the net will appear." On the first day of the new year, I quit my day job to follow my heart and devote more time to writing and teaching. I developed a writing workshop business, one in which I have been able to create supportive, encouraging environments for women to write their stories and become empowered and healed in the process. It is through this work that I do my part to create a more gentle and loving planet. I have been able to creatively express myself through the publication of my work and the successful direction of theatrical productions. And I rode my bicycle 300 miles across the state of Michigan for the fourth year in a row with my daughter and sister, and became a certified sailor—all empowering and joyous events layered in among the sorrows of life.

I see more clearly now that it's true—life really is short, and we need to be awake for all of it, to face our sorrows with open eyes and heart, and not shy away from the pain. We need to grieve our losses and then go on. Recognizing that sometimes it is only our sense of humor that helps us through, I laugh at life's absurdities. What else could I do when, after dragging the bathroom door outside for a paint job, sanding and painting it, then sanding and painting it again after rain ruined the first coat, then sanding and painting it *again*, I realized I had sanded and painted the wrong side of the door! It's the side that now stands out like a blazing snowdrift among the brown doors it keeps company with in the narrow hallway, and I laugh every time I see it.

We need to look for joy anywhere we can find it. I keep a gratitude journal next to my bed to record my simple joys: the crunchy Michigan leaves my sister gathers and sends to me each fall, knowing they take me home again; the dark, rainy weekends that signal the advent of winter and turn me inward to express the words written on my heart.

Recognizing that we are our own best friends, I make time to do things that nurture my spirit. I enjoy solitude, and walk my dog Buddy down our country road, catching his excitement at what we might see today. I explore the garden and discover what surprises await me, maybe some plant I had given up on that tenaciously held on and bloomed yet another year. Prayer and meditation are my daily ritual. I seek spiritual grace in my daily life, aware that I am but a small part of a much larger picture. These things nurture my soul. I make time to write, knowing that this processing of my life through words nourishes and heals me, and that I get cranky if I don't allow time for it. I think writing is about paying attention, so I notice and savor ordinary moments—the smell of freshly washed sheets hung on the line or the way the light comes through the window and illuminates the white tulips in my mother's blue vase.

We women possess valuable jewels in our women friends; they help us through many joys and sorrows and give us the opportunity to become our best selves. In times of adversity, it is the strength of our women friends upon which we can draw and who stay the course with us. Working to break free of fear and unrealistic expectations, we can continually seek ways to live a more spiritual life with love, compassion, and harmony at its core.

Always, I stay connected to my Creator. My faith is the most important relationship I tend to in this life. I remind myself that the past and the future are not in our hands. Above all, I remember that life, for each of us, is a precious gift, every ordinary moment of it.

Jane Foley

Epilogue

EACH WOMAN IN THIS BOOK TOOK A DIFFERENT PATH to her moment of midlife clarity. Your own arrival at that moment is a function of so many factors: the gene pool you emerged from, your environmental influences, and the way you react to both. As we grow, our lives change, sometimes randomly, sometimes deliberately, creating our own reality.

I am an ultrasound technologist. One day, as I scanned a seventy-two-year-old man—an author and poet, we began talking about life and books and dreams. I have had prophetic dreams since I was a child, and my scientific mind has always struggled to understand them.

I explained to my patient how I might dream of a plane crash and then, the next day, may see on the news that an actual plane had crashed. As I recall my dream, I find that all the information about the actual event was presented to me in the dream, albeit in a slightly confused scenario.

He watched me as I spoke, studying my words, and then asked, "Who is to say the dream is what is confused?"

I thought for a long while. "Wow, I have never once considered that the dream was the accurate piece of information and the reality may be confused."

He smiled one of those all-knowing smiles of a very wise man and continued, "Look through a kaleidoscope. An array of colorful pieces lies at its base. Turn the end and look again. What do you see? Confusion? Has anything been added or subtracted? Every piece is exactly the same, yet the look, the reality, is considerably different as you turn its base. Just as your dreams have all the pieces for you to see, so does life. It's up to you to decide what is reality and what is confusion."

I thought about this analogy for days. I looked in the mirror. Did I see confusion? No, I saw someone whose hair was messed up, who needed to lose a few pounds, who could use an update to that same old make-up routine. All the pieces were there, just as in the kaleidoscope. Turn it, I thought. It's so easy.

Finding clarity necessitates turning the end of your own kaleidoscope. The pieces are all there. The same pieces that were there the last time you looked in the mirror, or last year or last decade, or when you last felt overwhelmed by life.

Your moment of midlife clarity—the realization that you are surrounded by life—is the moment when you learn that you are in control of turning your own kaleidoscope and, ultimately, your own destiny.

OTHER BOOKS FROM
BEYOND WORDS PUBLISHING, INC.

Our Turn, Our Time
Women Truly Coming of Age
Editor: Cynthia Black; Foreword: Christina Baldwin
$14.95, softcover

Our Turn, Our Time is an amazing collection of essays written by women who are committed to celebrating and valuing their passages into the second half of life. These women are redefining the role older women play in contemporary society by embracing creativity, spirituality, and sisterhood. These essays are filled with insight, humor, and compassion on a broad variety of topics: the richness of women's groups, the rewards of volunteering, the power of crone ceremonies, the fires of creative expression, the challenges of a changing body, and the confidence that comes from success in later life.

Rites of Passage
Celebrating Life's Changes
Authors: Kathleen Wall, Ph.D., and Gary Ferguson
$12.95, softcover

Every major transition in our lives—be it marriage, high-school graduation, the death of a parent or spouse, or the last child leaving home—brings with it opportunities for growth and self-actualization and for repositioning ourselves in the world. Personal ritual—the focus of Rites of Passage—allows us to use the energy held within the anxiety of change to nourish the new person that is forever struggling to be born. Rites of Passage begins by explaining to readers that human growth is not linear, as many of us assume, but rather occurs in a five-part cycle. After sharing the patterns of transition, the authors then show the reader how ritual can help him or her move through these specific life changes: work and career, intimate relationships, friends, divorce, changes within the family, adolescence, issues in the last half of life, and personal loss.

The Woman's Book of Dreams
Dreaming as a Spiritual Practice
Author: Connie Cockrell Kaplan; Foreword: Jamie Sams
$14.95, softcover

Dreams are the windows to your future and the catalysts to bringing the new and creative into your life. Everyone dreams. Understanding the power of dreaming helps you achieve your greatest potential with ease. *The Woman's Book of Dreams* emphasizes the uniqueness of women's dreaming and shows the reader how to dream with intention, clarity, and focus. In addition, this book will teach you how to recognize the thirteen types of dreams, how your monthly cycles affect your dreaming, how the moon's position in the sky and its relationship to your astrological chart determine your dreaming, and how to track your dreams and create a personal map of your dreaming patterns. Connie Kaplan guides you through an ancient woman's group form called dream circle—a sacred space in which to share dreams with others on a regular basis. Dream circle allows you to experience life's mystery by connecting with other dreamers. It shows you that through dreaming together with your circle, you create the reality in which you live. It is time for you to recognize the power of dreams and to put yours into action. This book will inspire you to do all that—and more.

Pride and Joy
The Lives and Passions of Women Without Children
Author: Terri Casey
$14.95, softcover

Pride and Joy is an enlightening collection of first-person interviews with twenty-five women who have decided not to have children. This book shatters the stereotypes that surround voluntarily childless women—that they are self-centered, immature, workaholic, unfeminine, materialistic, child-hating, cold, or neurotic. Diversity is a strong suit of this book. The narrators range in age from twenty-six-year-old Sarah Klein, who teaches second grade in an inner-city public school, to eighty-two-year-old Ruby Burton, a retired court reporter who grew up in a mining camp. The women talk about their family histories, intimate relationships, self-images, creative outlets, fears, ambitions, dreams, and connections to the next generation. Even though these women are not mothers, many voluntarily childless women help to raise and sometimes rescue the next generation while retaining the personal freedom they find so integral to their identities.

The Second Wives Club
Secrets for Becoming Lovers for Life
Authors: Lenore Fogelson Millian, Ph.D., and
Stephen Jerry Millian, Ph.D.
$14.95, softcover

Are you or someone you know a second wife? Are you tired of arguing about your husband's first marriage? *The Second Wives Club* is the book you've been waiting for. Join the Club and learn the six secrets of successful second marriages. Learn how you can have wedded bliss while avoiding the pitfalls that second marriages bring. Don't be put off by his ex-wife. Help him get rid of his old "baggage" and make space in your relationship to be lovers for life. Includes chapters on how to deal with the first wife, the children, the grandchildren, the mother-in-law, the friends, and the memories.

Celebrating Time Alone
Stories of Splendid Solitude
Author: Lionel Fisher
$14.95, softcover

Celebrating Time Alone, with its profiles in solitude, shows us how to be magnificently alone through a celebration of our self: the self that can get buried under mountains of information, appointments, and activities. Lionel Fisher interviewed men and women across the country who have achieved great emotional clarity by savoring their individuality and solitude. In a writing style that is at once eloquent and down to earth, the author interweaves their real-life stories with his own insights and experiences to offer counsel, inspiration, and affirmation on living well alone.

The Intuitive Way
A Guide to Living from Inner Wisdom
Author: Penney Peirce; Foreword: Carol Adrienne
$16.95, softcover

When intuition is in full bloom, life takes on a magical, effortless quality; your world is suddenly full of synchronicities, creative insights, and abundant knowledge just for the asking. *The Intuitive Way* shows you how to enter that state of perceptual aliveness and integrate it into daily life to achieve greater natural flow through an easy-to-understand, ten-step course. Author Penney Peirce synthesizes teachings from psychology, East-West philosophy, religion, metaphysics, and business. In simple and direct language, Peirce describes the intuitive process as a new way of life and demonstrates many practical applications from speeding decision-making to expanding personal growth. Whether you're just beginning to search for a richer, fuller life experience or are looking for more subtle, sophisticated insights about your spiritual path, *The Intuitive Way* will be your companion as you progress through the stages of intuition development.

PowerHunch!
Living an Intuitive Life
Author: Marcia Emery, Ph.D.; Foreword: Leland Kaiser, Ph.D.
$15.95, softcover

Whether it's relationships, career, balance and healing, or simple everyday decision-making, intuition gives everyone an edge. In *PowerHunch!* Dr. Emery is your personal trainer as you develop your intuitive muscle. She shows you how to consistently and accurately apply your hunches to any problem and offers countless examples of intuition in action, covering a wide spectrum of occupations and relationships. With its intriguing stories and expert advice, *PowerHunch!* gives you the necessary tools and principles to create an intuitive life for yourself.

Teach Only Love
The Twelve Principles of Attitudinal Healing
Author: Gerald G. Jampolsky, M.D.
$12.95, softcover

From best-selling author Dr. Gerald Jampolsky comes a revised and expanded version of one of his classic works, based on *A Course in Miracles*. In 1975, Dr. Jampolsky founded the Center for Attitudinal Healing, a place where children and adults with life-threatening illnesses could practice peace of mind as an instrument of spiritual transformation and inner healing—practices that soon evolved into an approach to life with profound benefits for everyone. This book explains the twelve principles developed at the Center, all of which are based on the healing power of love, forgiveness, and oneness. They provide a powerful guide that allows all of us to heal our relationships and bring peace and harmony to every aspect of our lives.

Forgiveness
The Greatest Healer of All
Author: Gerald G. Jampolsky, M.D.; Foreword: Neale Donald Walsch
$12.95, softcover

Forgiveness: The Greatest Healer of All is written in simple, down-to-earth language. It explains why so many of us find it difficult to forgive and why holding on to grievances is really a decision to suffer. The book describes what causes us to be unforgiving and how our minds work to justify this. It goes on to point out the toxic side effects of being unforgiving and the havoc it can play on our bodies and on our lives. But above all, it leads us to the vast benefits of forgiving.

The author shares powerful stories that open our hearts to the miracles which can take place when we truly believe that no one needs to be excluded from our love. Sprinkled throughout the book are Forgiveness Reminders that may be used as daily affirmations supporting a new life free of past grievances.

The Great Wing
A Parable
Author: Louis A. Tartaglia, M.D.; Foreword: Father Angelo Scolozzi
$14.95, hardcover

The Great Wing transforms the timeless miracle of the migration of a flock of geese into a parable for the modern age. It recounts a young goose's own reluctant but steady transformation from gangly fledgling to Grand Goose and his triumph over the turmoils of his soul and the buffeting of a mighty Atlantic storm. In *The Great Wing*, our potential as individuals is affirmed, as is the power of group prayer, or the "Flock Mind." As we make the journey with this goose and his flock, we rediscover that we tie our own potential into the power of the common good by way of attributes such as honesty, hope, courage, trust, perseverance, spirituality, and service. The young goose's trials and tribulations, as well as his triumph, are our own.

There's a Hole in My Sidewalk
The Romance of Self-Discovery
Author: Portia Nelson
$7.95, softcover

This classic, well-loved guide to life is warm, wise, and funny. Portia Nelson's book and her poem "Autobiography in Five Short Chapters" have been embraced by individuals, therapy groups, and self-help programs around the world.

When God Winks
How the Power of Concidence Guides Your Life
Author: SQuire Rushnell
$16.95, hardcover

When God Winks confirms a belief secretly held by most readers: there is more to coincidences than meets the eye. Like winks from a loving grandparent, coincidences are messages from above that you are not alone and everything will be OK. The compelling theory of why coincidences exist is applied to fascinating stories in history, sports, the news, medicine, and relationships involving both everyday people and celebrities.

The Infinite Thread
Healing Relationships beyond Loss
Author: Alexandra Kennedy
$14.95, softcover

The death of a loved one is often accompanied by regrets—for what we said or didn't say, what we did or didn't do. In our grief, our old resentments, regrets, and unexpressed love can hinder our emotional growth, creating wounds that affect all our other relationships. With exercises designed to re-create and heal past relationships, *The Infinite Thread* illustrates that keeping our loved one alive in our hearts—and in our minds—will enable us to make peace with the past and move freely into the future.

To order or to request a catalog, contact
Beyond Words Publishing, Inc.
20827 N.W. Cornell Road, Suite 500
Hillsboro, OR 97124-9808
503-531-8700 or 1-800-284-9673

You can also visit our Web site at *www.beyondword.com*
or e-mail us at *info@beyondword.com*.

BEYOND WORDS PUBLISHING, INC.

OUR CORPORATE MISSION

Inspire to Integrity

OUR DECLARED VALUES

We give to all of life as life has given us.
We honor all relationships.
Trust and stewardship are integral to fulfilling dreams.
Collaboration is essential to create miracles.
Creativity and aesthetics nourish the soul.
Unlimited thinking is fundamental.
Living your passion is vital.
Joy and humor open our hearts to growth.
It is important to remind ourselves of love.